50 SIMPLE THINGS KIDS CAN DO TO RECYCLE

The EarthWorks Group

Illustrations by Michele Montez

EarthWorks Press
Berkeley, CA

THIS BOOK IS PRINTED ON RECYCLED PAPER

To the very young. So she'll have a choice.

Created and Packaged by Javnarama
Designed by Javnarama
Layout by Fritz Springmeyer
Illustrations by Michele Montez
Cover design by Jean Sanchirico

Acknowledgments

*John Javna & The EarthWorks Group would like to thank
everyone who helped make this book possible, including:*

- Sven Newman
- Linda Allison
- Gordon Javna
- Linda Glaser
- Fritz Springmeyer
- Michele Montez
- Lenna Lebovich
- Rob Dewey
- Nancy Skinner

- Lyn Speakman
- Julie Roeming
- Paul Stanley
- Joanne Miller
- Phil Catalfo
- Stuart Greenbaum
- Ecology Action
- Piet Canin
- Susan Allen

- Rob Williams
- Julie Bennett
- Nenelle Bunnin
- Christopher Williams
- Steve Lautze
- John Dollison
- Melissa Schwarz
- Portia Sinnot

*...and a host of other contributors who've lent a hand
during the 3-1/2 years we've worked on this book.*

CONTENTS

INTRODUCTION

I n 1990, the Earthworks Group (that's us) wrote our first book for kids—*50 Simple things Kids Can Do to Save the Earth.*

To our surprise, it became the biggest- selling children's environmental book ever written! Millions of kids around the world read it...and a lot of them have written to us.

And what do you think they write about most often?

Recycling.

We've gotten thousands of letters like these:

"Dear EarthWorks:
I like the idea of recycling to save the Earth. My mom says we can save newspapers at our house and recycle them. Is there anything else we can collect? "

"Dear Sir/Madam:
I totally love your book. It is wonderful and I, being a Girl Scout and my mother being the co-leader, made it even more interesting. In fact, a few days ago my Girl Scout troop visited the Miami Recycling Plant. We learned that you can recycle plastics—which we didn't know! We also had been collecting clear, colorless plastic and saving it up so when we went to the plant they could recycle it. We wound up with 88 pounds of plastic!
Now I'd love to see a sequel of your book."

"Dear Kids' EarthWorks Group:
I'm 11 years old and going onto 6th grade. I am very 'into' the environment. This year at our school, I started all the

5th grade classes recycling our paper. I live in Great Falls, Montana, and I am very proud of our city and state."

"Dear EarthWorks Group:
   My friends Zach, Chris and I are opening a recycling stand! We want our dads to help us build a stand! Well anyway, other than your wonderful *50 Simple Things Kids Can Do to Save the Earth* book, we would very much like you to write back telling us some things we should think about doing before we open it this summer!"

"Dear EarthWorks Group:
   Hello. My name is Suzanne and I'm ten years old. I'm writing this letter because I want to tell you a couple of things about recycling. My group in school is working on a newspaper about recycling, It's by Ryan, Libby, Christine, Scott, Cheryl, and me (and don't forget Tim). Each person has their own special job. We're writing it so that we can help 'spread the word.'"

   So when we decided to do another *50 Simple Things* book for kids, it seemed pretty clear that it should be about recycling.

   We've tried to make this book easy and fun to read, but we've also packed it with lots of information and ideas. It doesn't include everything about recycling...but it's a great start.

   Most of all, we want you to know that you have the power to change the world—to make our Earth a better place to live. There's a lot to do—and YOU are the one to do it.

**Recycling Is Saving the Earth...
a Little Bit at a Time.**

RECYCLING
BASICS

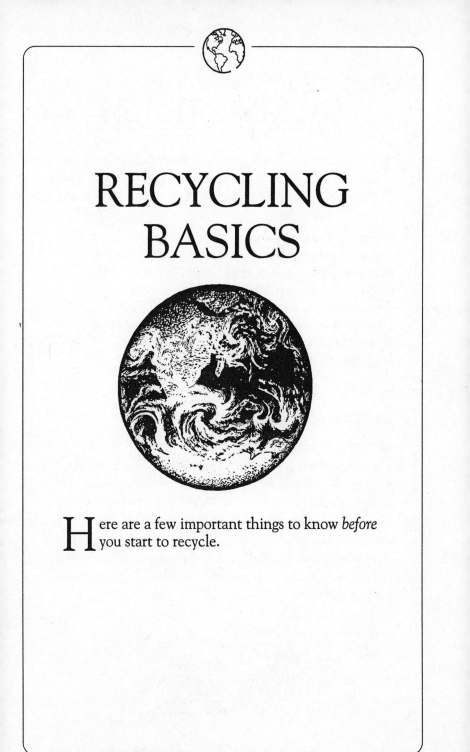

H ere are a few important things to know *before*
you start to recycle.

TALKING TRASH

I f you're like most kids, you don't think much about garbage. Even if it's your job to take out the trash, you probably just lug the garbage bag out to the trash can…dump it…and forget about it.

But have you ever stopped to think that *every day* someone in *every* family in America probably does the same thing? Believe it or not, the average American family throws away about ten pounds of garbage each day. In fact, if you combined all the garbage that all the families in the United States throw out in one year, you would have enough to fill a line of garbage trucks 145,000 miles long—more than halfway from here to the moon!

What happens to all that garbage?

WHERE DOES GARBAGE GO?

Most of our garbage is either burned or buried.

• If your garbage is going to be burned, it is hauled off to a giant oven called an *incinerator*. Inside the incinerator, trash is cooked until all that's left is *ash*. In this country, about one-tenth of all garbage ends up at an incinerator.

• More likely, your trash is heading for a dump. In the old days, dumps were just big holes in the ground; when they were filled with trash, they were covered with dirt to keep out rats and flies.

- Modern dumps are called *landfills*. They are still big holes in the ground, but now they're lined with plastic or clay, to keep the garbage from touching the bottom and sides of the hole (like giant plastic garbage bags).

- After garbage trucks dump trash in little sections of the landfill, the garbage is smashed flat with a bulldozer and covered with soil.

- When a landfill is full, it is closed, and grass is planted on top. It might become a park area.

THE PROBLEMS WITH LANDFILLS

- Right now there are about 5,200 landfills in America. But that's still not enough to hold all our garbage. Many of those landfills are *already* full, and many more will be full soon.

- That means we need to find new places to put garbage. This is a problem, because it takes a lot of space to create a landfill—space that could be used for parks, schools…or just left as wilderness for people and animals to enjoy. And even if we can find the space, we still have a problem—nobody wants a landfill in *their* backyard.

- There are other problems, too: Landfills can be very unhealthy. When rain falls on landfills, water mixes with garbage to form a poisonous "soup" called *leachate*. Leachate can leak into the ground, and if we're not careful, that garbage "soup" may seep right into the water we drink!

WHAT ABOUT INCINERATORS?

- Burning seems like a neat solution. But there are problems with that, too. For one thing, incinerators are *very* expensive to build and run.

- For another, burning doesn't actually *get rid* of our garbage. About 2/3 of the trash that's incinerated goes up in smoke…which creates air pollution.

• The stuff that is left—the other 1/3 of the trash—turns into ash, which *still* must be buried or stored somewhere. But that is not the end of the problem; the ash is often *toxic*—which means it's poisonous and dangerous to our health, too.

THE SOLUTIONS

You can see there are some big problems with dumping our garbage in landfills or burning it in incinerators. But what else can we do with it?

Well, suppose we just made less garbage by buying fewer things that had to be thrown away?

That's called *Reducing*.

And suppose that instead of throwing things away as soon as we were done with them, we used them again—or gave them to someone who would?

That's called *Reusing*.

And suppose, instead of just throwing things like cans and bottles away, we brought them to people who would turn them into useful new products again?

That's called *Recycling*.

Together, these solutions are called the "Three R's"...and they are what this book is all about.

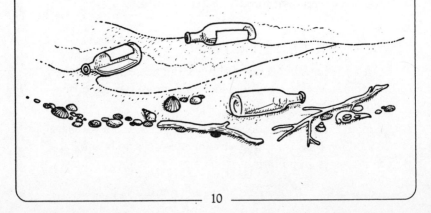

THE THREE R's

I f you want to help solve our garbage problem, you need to know the Three R's.

REDUCE

You can cut down on garbage *before* you buy something.

 For example, when you're picking out an item at the store, take the time to think about what you'll be able to reuse or recycle, and what you'll have to toss in the trash. Reducing means throwing away less.

According to Bobbie Kalman in her book, *Reducing, Reusing & Recycling,* "One of the best ways to cut down on the amount we waste is to stop buying things we don't need in the first place. This means that we have to pay attention when we go to the store to shop."

REUSE

A book you've finished, a plastic bag, a cottage cheese container, an old toy, a sweater you've outgrown—none of these thing *have* to be thrown away. You can keep them out of landfills by either reusing them yourself or by passing them on to somebody else who can reuse them.

Reusing means saving things that would usually be thrown out, and using them over again.

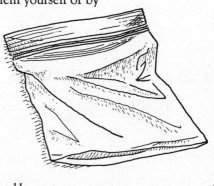

RECYCLE

Of course there are some things you can't reuse, like empty aluminum cans or last year's phone book. But the *materials* they are made of can be used over and over again by *recycling* them.

Instead of tossing aluminum cans, glass bottles, paper, cardboard, plastic soda bottles, and other recyclables into the trash, you can take them to a recycling center. The recycling center sorts the materials and sends them to factories, which make new products that people will use again.

✓ Recycling is turning used paper into pulp and then making new paper from that pulp.

✓ Recycling is crushing used glass bottles into little pieces and melting them to make new glass products.

✓ Recycling is melting used aluminum cans, pressing the melted metal into sheets, and shaping these sheets into new cans or other aluminum products.

✓ Recycling is shredding and melting used plastic bottles to make carpet.

In other words, recycling is turning something old into something new. And that's like getting something for free.

ALL ABOUT RECYCLING

We know that recycling is the best way to deal with our garbage. After all, what could be better than taking things we can't use anymore—like yesterday's newspaper or an empty soda can—and turning them into new and useful things—like recycled paper or a new aluminum can?

Unfortunately, right now Americans are only recycling about 10%-15% of all our garbage.

But there is good news—experts say that we *could* recycle almost all of our garbage. We just need people like *you* to get us started.

WHY RECYCLE?
Taking things that would be garbage and reusing them is a great way to help the Earth. You already know why it's good to keep garbage out of landfills and incinerators. But there are a lot of other reasons to recycle, too:

It saves natural resources.
The things we use every day—newspapers, soda cans, plastic bottles—are made from materials that come from the Earth. We get newspaper from trees. We get soda cans from metal we dig out of the Earth. And we get plastic from oil we pump out of the Earth.

Our planet has a limited supply of these precious resources, but we keep treating them like garbage.

For example:

• *Every hour of the day*, Americans throw out 2.5 million plastic beverage bottles! That's enough to circle the earth four times in a year.

• *Every week*, we throw out more than 500 million glass bottles and jars—enough to fill a huge skyscraper from the basement to the top floor.

• *Every three months* we throw out enough aluminum to rebuild all the planes in America's airlines.

• *Every year*, we throw out enough white writing paper to build a 12-foot-high wall of paper all the way across the country, from New York to Los Angeles.

By recycling we can save these resources instead. Rather than taking more new materials from the Earth, we will use the same materials over and over again.

Recycling saves energy.
Energy is one of the most valuable things on Earth. It is the power to make cars go, to create heat and light, to make things in factories, and so on. We get this energy from the Earth's resources, by burning coal, oil, or natural gas to generate electricity.

It takes a lot of energy to dig metal out of the Earth...chop down a forest of trees...or get oil from the ground. And it takes a lot of energy to turn these *raw materials* into products in a factory.

So recycling saves energy in two ways: It lets us reuse materials, instead of wasting the energy it would take to get them from the Earth all over again; and it allows factories to use less energy, because recycled materials are easier to turn into new products than raw materials are.

For example:

• It takes 20 times more energy to make an aluminum can from new materials than from recycled materials.

• Every year, we save enough energy by recycling steel to supply the city of Los Angeles with electricity for ten years!

• Making paper and glass out of recycled materials uses more than 25% less energy than making them from new materials.

Recycling creates less pollution.
Making products from *any* kind of materials creates pollution. As factories run, for instance, pollution is put into the air through their smokestacks. Chemicals used to make paper or plastic can get into our lakes and rivers and pollute them.

If we want new products, there is always going to be *some* pollution. But we can have less pollution if we use recycled materials.

For example:

• Making an aluminum can from recycled materials creates 95% less air pollution than making it from raw materials.

• For every ton (2,000 pounds) of paper we recycle, we keep 7,000 gallons of water from being treated with chemicals.

• Making glass out of recycled materials cuts air pollution by 14%-20%.

So, recycling helps keep our air and water clean. That's good for people, plants, and animals.

Recycling protects animals.

When we make holes for landfills...dig for metal or oil...cut down trees...pollute our water or air, we threaten the places where wild animals live—their *habitats*.

Recycling means less digging and drilling...less cutting and dumping...and less destruction of forests, rivers, and fields.

Recycling helps our communities.

It may sound kind of funny, but garbage is expensive. We have to pay for people to come by in trucks to pick up our garbage, we have to pay to build landfills to keep garbage in, and we have to pay people to run the landfills.

If we create less garbage, our communities can save money. That means more money could be spent on other things— like building playgrounds, buying library books, or improving schools.

LEARN WHAT YOU CAN RECYCLE

T he things we use each day are made of many different materials. Some are recyclable, some aren't.

This section will teach you about the most common recyclables—what they are, and how you can recycle them.

Take a few minutes to learn more about them—it will make you a much better recycler.

1. A CLEAR CHOICE

Take a Guess.
How many times can you recycle a glass bottle?
A) *Once* **B)** *25 times* **C)** *An unlimited number of times*

You may not realize it, but there's something in your refrigerator that's so old, George Washington or Abraham Lincoln could have used it.

Is it last week's leftovers? That weird, moldy green stuff in a bowl? Nope. It's the *glass* in the bottles and jars.

Believe it or not, people have been using—and *recycling*—glass for almost 3,000 years! Now you can be part of that history by recycling *your* empty bottles and jars, too.

RECYCLING FACTS

• Glass is usually made by mixing sand with a few other natural ingredients (soda, feldspar and limestone). The mixture is put into a very hot furnace and when it melts, it turns to glass. Heating the furnace takes a lot of energy.

• Glass can *also* be made by melting down *old* glass (such as bottles and jars). This is better for the Earth, because recycled glass melts at a lower temperature than new materials—so it takes less energy to heat the furnace.

• For example: Recycling just one bottle can save enough energy to light a 100-watt light bulb for 4 hours!

• Making glass from recycled jars and bottles creates less air pollution, too...and it uses fewer natural resources. For every

18

ton (that's 2,000 pounds) of glass that gets recycled, we save a ton of the raw materials it would take to make new glass.

HOW TO RECYCLE GLASS

• When you finish with a bottle or jar, lightly rinse it out with water. (You don't have to wash it with soap.) Leftover food or drinks attract ants and other pests.

• Don't forget to take off caps or lids. They can't be recycled with the glass. (If they're metal, recycle them with aluminum or steel. If they're plastic, throw them out.)

• It's okay to leave on paper and plastic labels—they burn or blow off when the glass is recycled.

• "Neck rings"—the part of the bottle caps that are still on the bottlenecks—can be left on, too.

• Wash off sand and dirt from bottles you find in parks, beaches, etc. Even one little stone can ruin a whole load of recycled glass!

RECYCLING TIPS

• Some recycling centers want you to keep different-colored glass (clear, brown, and green) in different recycling containers. Call your local center to find out *their* rules.

• Most glass bottles and jars can be recycled. *But you can't recycle windows, drinking glasses, vases, mirrors, or light bulbs.* They're made of different kinds of glass that can't be melted down with bottles and jars.

• Want to find out more about glass recycling? Write to *The Glass Packaging Institute*, 1627 K St. NW, Suite 800, Washington, DC 20006.

2. DON'T CAN IT!

Take a Guess.
How many aluminum cans does an
average American use in a year?
A) 10   **B)** 150   **C)** 320

What can people do with soda cans after the soda's gone? You might be surprised: they can make airplane parts with them...or use them in new bicycles...or turn them into frying pans.

How? By recycling them.

Soda cans are made of a valuable metal called aluminum. It's used in everything from space shuttles to pie pans.

Americans already recycle more than 60 billion aluminum cans a year. But we need *your* cans, too.

RECYCLING FACTS

• Here's how aluminum is recycled: Soda cans, beer cans, and other aluminum products (like pie pans and aluminum foil) are sent to factories, where they're ground into little metal chips.

• Then they're melted down and turned into solid aluminum bars.

• The bars are rolled into sheets of aluminum, which are sold to can makers, who make new cans out of them.

• There's no limit to the number of times aluminum can be melted down and reused. The can you're drinking out of today might actually have been part of someone else's soda can 20 years ago...and, if you recycle it, it could be part of

Answer: C. Almost one a day!

someone else's soda can 20 years from now.

• Recycling saves energy as well as aluminum. For example: The energy you save by recycling just one aluminum can could keep your TV running for 3 hours!

HOW TO RECYCLE ALUMINUM

• Rinse out empty cans, so leftover soda doesn't attract bugs.

• Clean food off aluminum foil, pie pans, and TV dinner trays. Note: Some recycling centers want "other aluminum" (pie pans, foil, etc.) separated from the cans. Be sure to check with your center before recycling them.

• To save space, some people crush their aluminum cans. However, not all recycling centers will take crushed cans, so check first.

RECYCLING TIPS

• If you're not sure a can is aluminum, do the "magnet test." Hold a magnet up to it. If the magnet sticks, the can is steel, not aluminum. If it doesn't stick, it's aluminum.

• Some cans, called "bi-metal," are made with an aluminum top and steel sides. So be sure to check the top, bottom *and* sides with a magnet. Bi-metal cans are usually recycled with steel cans (see p. 32).

• Almost all recycling centers take aluminum cans. But "buyback centers" will even pay you money for them! Check the yellow pages to see if there's one near you.

• To find out more about recycling aluminum, write to *The Aluminum Association*, 900 19th St. NW, Suite 300, Washington, DC 20006

3. IT'S OLD NEWS

Take a Guess.
What can be made from recycled newspapers?
A) *Cereal boxes* **B)** *Construction paper* **C)** *More newspapers*

Stop the presses!
Here's some important recycling news: "Experts have discovered that newspapers take up more space in our landfills than any other item!"

You can help fight this garbage problem—and save millions of trees at the same time.

How? By recycling newspapers instead of throwing them away.

RECYCLING FACTS
• Experts say that Americans buy an average of 62 million newspapers every day—and throw away 44 million of them! That means we throw out as many as 500,000 trees' worth of newspapers *every week.*

• But we can save trees instead, because the paper used in these newspapers—called "newsprint"—can be recycled.

• Factories recycle newspapers by adding water and chemicals to them, then stirring the mixture into a kind of "soup."

Answer: A, B, C. Newspapers can also become egg cartons, insulation, and lots more!

- Next, they put the "soup" into paper-making machines that spray it across big screens and dry it with hot air. When it comes out, it's ready to be used in newspapers again.
- Recycling newspapers cuts air pollution and saves energy. For example: It takes half as much energy to recycle newsprint as it takes to make newsprint fresh from trees.

HOW TO RECYCLE

- Almost any recycling center will take newspapers.
- Some want newspapers tied into bundles with string. Others want them stacked in boxes or paper bags. Call your local center to see what they prefer.
- If you have to tie newspapers, here's an easy way to do it:
    ✓ Lay two pieces of string on the floor in a cross.
    ✓ Put a small stack of papers (about a foot high) on top, pull the strings up, and tie them in a knot.

RECYCLING TIPS

- Anything that comes with the newspaper (shiny colored pages, store ads, etc.) can be recycled. But don't add anything extra. "Junk mail" or magazines must be recycled separately (see p. 30).
- If you've used newspaper for art projects or to line your pet hamster's cage, don't recycle it—throw it out.
- Want to find out more about newspaper recycling? Write to *The Newspaper Association of America*, 11600 Sunrise Valley Drive, Reston, VA 22091. Attn: Communications Dept.

4. BRIGHT WHITE

Take a Guess.
*What can you do with an old piece of notebook paper before
you recycle it?* **A)** *Build a house* **B)** *Make a shoelace*
C) *Use the other side*

You're writing a report for school…and your pen slips.

Arghh!…It looks like you've got to start over again!

So you crumple up the old sheet of paper and start to toss it in the trash.

But wait!

Did you know that piece of white paper is still worth something? In fact, some recyclers say it's the most valuable paper there is.

RECYCLING FACTS

• What's "white paper"? Writing paper, notebook paper, white envelopes, typing paper, index cards, computer paper, copier paper, and white stationery.

• Why is it more valuable than other kinds of paper?

✓ The little "strings" of wood that hold it together, called *fibers*, are shorter and stronger than the fibers in most other paper…so it makes better paper when it's recycled.

Answer: C. Why throw a piece of paper away when it's only half used?

✓ To make paper white, manufacturers usually add bleach —a chemical that causes pollution. But "white paper" doesn't need to be bleached when it's recycled—it's *already* bleached. So recyclers don't have to add as many chemicals. This cuts water pollution.

• Recycling white paper saves energy, too. It takes 1/3 less energy to make recycled white paper than it does to make it from new materials.

HOW TO RECYCLE

• Most white paper needs no special attention for recycling, but here are a few things you should watch out for.

   ✓ *Stickers and "post-it" notes*: These can't be recycled with white paper. If they're attached to white paper, pull them off.

   ✓ *Paper clips*: Staples can be left on white paper, but it's a good idea to take off paper clips.

   ✓ *Envelopes*: White envelopes can be recycled as white paper. But first, tear out plastic "windows" and pull off any stick-on labels.

RECYCLING TIPS

• Before you take your white paper to a recycling center, reuse it at home. Use the clean side for notes, lists, pictures, and so on (see p. 56).

• Remember: It's important to keep white paper separate from other paper when you recycle it.

5. CORRUGATED CARDBOARD

Take a Guess.
What's the best thing to do with a box when you're done with it?
A) *Eat it for breakfast* **B)** *Eat it for lunch* **C)** *Recycle it*

How many big, brown cardboard boxes do you have in your house? Are there some stacked in your closet with old clothes in them? Do you have a few stashed under your bed, full of toys, books, or secret papers?

These cardboard boxes are valuable when you're using them…and they're also valuable when you're done with them, because they can be recycled into new boxes—which saves trees and energy and fights pollution.

DID YOU KNOW

• Some cardboard boxes are so strong, they can hold more than 100 pounds without breaking.

• Why? Because each piece of cardboard is really three layers of thick paper glued together like a sandwich.

• The layer in the middle is strongest because it is made up of a thick piece of paper that is folded into a lot of little

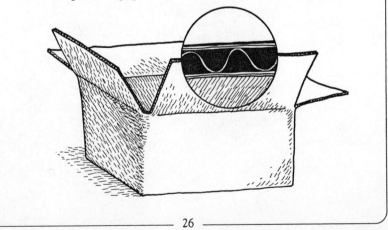

Answer: C. If you answered A or B, *please* don't invite us to your house to eat.

ridges. Those ridges are called *corrugation*... and that's why it's called *corrugated cardboard*.

• Making corrugated boxes with recycled cardboard takes just 1/4 of the energy and creates only 1/2 as much pollution as making them from new materials!

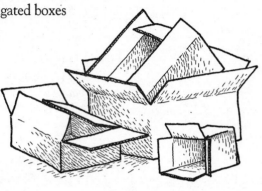

• To recyclers, cereal boxes, shoe boxes, and cracker boxes are not considered cardboard. The paper they're made of is called *paperboard*. It can't be recycled with corrugated cardboard, but it *can* be recycled with "mixed paper" (see p. 30.)

HOW TO RECYCLE CARDBOARD

• Remove as much plastic, tape, and labels from cardboard boxes as you can. They can gum up the recycling machines.

• Take out anything that's still inside your boxes—like foam packing, string, or plastic.

• Cardboard boxes take up a lot of space. But it's easier to store them if you flatten them. Here's how to do it:

✓ Pull open all the flaps on both ends of the box.

✓ When the flaps are open, put the box on its side and push down. It should fold flat.

• If you keep one box open, you can store all the flattened boxes standing up inside of it, like files in a filing cabinet.

Note: Brown paper bags are made of the same kind of paper as cardboard, so you may be able to recycle them with cardboard boxes. Check with your recycling center.

6. CALLING ALL PHONE BOOKS

Take a Guess.
Which one of these can't be made out
of recycled phone books?
A) *Book covers* **B)** *Ceiling tiles* **C)** *Big Macs*

What book does your family use the most: The dictionary? The encyclopedia? The phone book?

It's probably the phone book.

Think of all the times you use it: when you want to get in touch with friends, when you're looking for a place to shop, when you need an address, and so on.

But as soon as the phone company sends you a new phone book, the old one becomes worthless...or does it? The fact is, you can still put it to good use—by recycling it.

PHONE BOOK RECYCLING

• Phone books are made from a very low-quality kind of paper called *groundwood*. Unfortunately, it's not strong

Answer: C. Who'd want to eat a Big Mac made of *paper*? Yecch.

enough to be recycled back into new paper.

• But groundwood can be recycled into many other useful things. For example: schoolbook covers, ceiling tiles, and even insulation to keep a home warm.

BE A RECYCLING DETECTIVE

• To recycle your phone books, there's only one thing you need to do—find someone who'll take them. Here are two places to check:

1. Your local recycling center. Some recycling centers take phone books with "mixed paper" (see p. 30).

2. Your local phone company. Some phone companies recycle old phone books as a service to customers. To find out if yours does, give them a call. Their "customer service" number is probably on your family's phone bill...or in the phone book.

• If the phone company doesn't recycle old phone books, it may be because they don't think it's worth the trouble. You can help to change their minds by writing a letter to let them know you think it's a good idea. (See p. 124 on writing letters).

7. MIXED PAPER

Take a Guess.
Which of these things can be recycled with mixed paper?
A) *Cement mix* **B)** *Ice cream* **C)** *Egg cartons*

Here's a trick recyclers do: They take a paper towel tube, an egg carton, and scraps of wrapping paper...mix them together...and Presto!—out comes a new cereal box.

Is it magic?

Nope. It's just another way recyclers have learned to reuse the Earth's resources.

And now, if a recycling center near you takes "mixed paper," you can help them...and help the Earth.

DID YOU KNOW

• "Mixed paper" is exactly what it sounds like—a mix of all different kinds of paper that aren't already being recycled by themselves.

Answer: C. Paper egg cartons are perfect for mixed-paper recycling.

• Mixed paper includes paper egg cartons, shoe boxes, cereal boxes, cracker boxes, toilet paper and paper towel tubes, the cardboard on the back of notepads, etc.

• "Junk mail"—those unwanted advertisements sent to your home in the mail—can be recycled with mixed paper, too.

• Mixed paper *can't* be recycled into high-quality writing paper, but it *can* be made into paperboard (the cardboard used in cereal boxes), and "roofing paper."

TO RECYCLE MIXED PAPER
Pay special attention to:

• **Cereal and cracker boxes:** Take plastic or wax paper out of boxes before you recycle them.

• **Egg cartons:** A little bit of egg is okay, but no eggshells.

• **Wrapping paper:** Take off as much tape as you can (little pieces are okay) and don't include string or ribbon. Paper with foil or plastic in it *cannot* be recycled.

• **Envelopes:** Rip out plastic windows and rip off stick-on labels before recycling.

• **Junk mail:** Be sure to open envelopes and take out any plastic or stickers before recycling it.

RECYCLING TIPS

• To save space, crush or fold bulky things like cereal boxes and egg cartons.

• "Mixed paper" doesn't include everything. Some paper can't be recycled at all: wax paper, tissues, paper towels, and paper cups and plates. (That's one reason it's good to use re-usable cloth dish towels and real cups and plates.)

• Before you recycle magazines as mixed paper, check to see if your recycler takes them separately.

• Remember: Not all recyclers take mixed paper yet. Before you start saving mixed paper, call your local centers to find out if anyone in your area wants it.

8. REAL STEEL

Take a Guess.
How can you tell if a can is made of steel? **A)** *Knock hard on*
it twice **B)** *Drop it and see if it bounces* **C)** *Use a magnet*

Next time you're in the supermarket, try counting all the cans on the shelves.

One...two...three...

Hey, wait a minute—this could take all day! There must be *thousands* of them.

That's right—and most of them are made of steel...so they *could* all be recycled.

Unfortunately, they probably won't be.

Why? Because people either don't know that steel cans are recyclable...or haven't found a recycler who will take them.

But here's some good news—if your local center takes them, recycling steel cans is easy.

RECYCLING FACTS

• Steel cans are also some-times called "tin cans." That's because a long time ago they were made out of a soft metal called "tin."

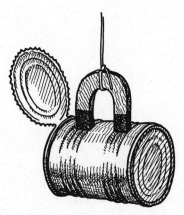

• Today a little bit of tin is used to coat each can, but most of the can is made of steel.

• When these cans are recy-cled, both the steel and the tin can be saved and reused to make cars, bridges, build-ings, bicycles, and many more things—including new cans.

Answer: C. Just checking to see if you'd already read page 21.

HOW TO RECYCLE STEEL CANS

• First, use a magnet to make sure the can is made of steel, not aluminum.

✓ If the magnet sticks to the can, it's steel.

✓ Be sure to check the top, bottom, and side of each can. Some cans are *bi-metal*—which means they're made of aluminum *and* steel. These usually get recycled with steel cans.

• Rinse out empty cans. (You can usually leave the labels on—ask your recycler.)

RECYCLING TIPS

• Steel cans are not as valuable to recyclers as aluminum cans right now, so not every recycling center will take them. Check with yours to see if they do.

• If they don't, look for a steel recycler in the yellow pages under "Scrap Metal." Or write to the Steel Can Recycling Institute at the address below. Ask for a list of steel-can recyclers in your area.

• *Recycling Resource:* For a learning sheet about steel recycling, write to the Steel Can Recycling Institute, Education Dept., Foster Plaza 10, 680 Andersen Drive, Pittsburgh, PA 15220. They have different ones for different ages, so tell them how old you are.

9. PET BOTTLES

Take a Guess.
What is a PET bottle?
A) *A bottle you keep on a leash*   **B)** *A plastic soda bottle*
C) *A bottle for your dog*

R iddle: When is a plastic soda bottle not a plastic soda bottle?

Answer: When it's a park bench.

That may sound crazy, but it's not. Recycled plastic soda bottles are actually melted down and turned into all kinds of new things you wouldn't expect: park benches, carpets, pillows, boat docks, paint brushes, and even clothes.

Many communities haven't started this kind of recycling yet. But if yours has, plastic is one more valuable thing you can recycle and keep out of a landfill.

DID YOU KNOW

• Plastic soda bottles, some detergent bottles, plastic peanut butter jars, and many other containers are made of a plastic called PET (or PETE).

• Why PET? It doesn't have anything to do with cats or dogs—it's short for *Polyethylene Terephthalate*.
Try saying *that* 3 times fast.

• How can you tell if a container is made of PET? Look on the bottom—if there's a recycling symbol with a #1 in the middle, it's PET.

Answer: Plastic soda bottles are made out of a plastic called PET.

Sometimes it says PET (or PETE), too.

• Recycled PET bottles are sent to factories, where they are shredded and turned into plastic flakes.

• Then the plastic flakes are used to make new products. For example, a PET soda bottle could be used in a suit made of a material called *polyester*...or the carpet in your home. (About one-third of all carpets in America contain recycled PET.)

• Want another example? Look at your winter jacket: if it has stuffing in it, you might be wearing part of a soda bottle—because PET is used to make *polyfill* stuffing, too.

HOW TO RECYCLE PET PLASTIC

Find out if you can recycle PET in your community. If so, then:

• Rinse out bottles and other PET containers.

• Take off the caps. Some PET containers come with aluminum caps. Those can be recycled with aluminum cans (see p. 20). Plastic caps have to be thrown away.

10. MILK JUGS

Take a Guess.
Where do old milk jugs wind up?
A) *Landfills*   **B)** *The forest*   **C)** *The ocean*

Here's something you might not know: Back in the 1950s and 1960s, many people didn't buy milk in stores.

Instead, a "milkman" stopped by their homes every few days to drop off glass bottles filled with milk. When the milk bottles were empty, the milkman picked them up so they could be used again.

Now things are different. Milk often comes in paper cartons (which can *sometimes* be recycled with "mixed paper") or in plastic jugs.

These plastic jugs can't be reused by the milk company. But in some communities they *can* be recycled.

DID YOU KNOW

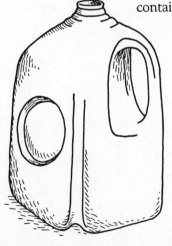

- Milk jugs are made of a type of plastic called HDPE (short for *high-density polyethylene*). Many other containers, such as butter tubs and detergent bottles, are also made of HDPE.

- Here's how HDPE is recycled: Factories shred it into little plastic flakes, which are cleaned with a vacuum, washed, and then dried.

- Then, the clean plastic flakes are sold to plastic companies, which melt them down and use them to make new plastic products.

Answer: All three, if we don't recycle them.

• So, the plastic milk jug you recycle *could* become someone's flower pot, soap bottle, plastic bucket...or even a recycling bin.

• How can you tell if a plastic container is made of HDPE? Look on the bottom. If there's a recycling symbol with a #2 in the middle, it's HDPE.

RECYCLING HDPE CONTAINERS

First, see if HDPE can be recycled in your area. If it can, then:

• Take off the caps. Throw them out. They're usually made of a different kind of plastic that can't be recycled.

• If there's a plastic ring on the neck of your milk jug (or other container), take it off, too.

• Some recyclers also want you to take off any labels. Check to find out.

• Rinse containers out (an especially good idea with milk jugs—sour milk makes plastic really smell gross).

• Want to save space? Stomp on milk jugs to flatten them.

RECYCLING TIPS

• Check with recyclers to see if clear HDPE can be mixed with colored HDPE containers .

• If you can't recycle HPDE containers in your town, find ways to reuse them, or think about buying things in other containers that *are* recyclable.

• In some areas, refillable glass milk bottles are making a comeback. Be a recycling detective—check your local supermarket for them.

11. OTHER PLASTICS

Take a Guess.
Which of these are sometimes made of plastic:
A) *Coat hangers* **B)** *Toys* **C)** *Picture frames*

Suppose scientists decided to dig up our garbage a thousand years from now. What would they find?

Well, they might discover some old televisions, refrigerators, car parts, bicycle tires…and *lots* of plastic—because plastic lasts a very long time—probably thousands of years.

Hm-m-m. If it's going to be around that long, maybe we should do something with it besides throwing it away—like using it again….and again…and again. That's why whenever you get the chance, it makes sense to try to recycle plastic.

HOW TO RECYCLE PLASTIC

• First, find out which plastics the recycling center in your community will take.

• Next, learn to identify the different kind of plastics. There are 6 kinds. You can tell them apart by looking for a recycling symbol with a number in it. Each plastic has a different number:

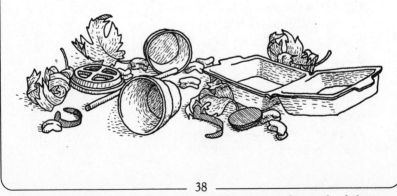

Answer: All of these—and thousands more things—are often made of plastic.

#1: PET (*polyethylene terephthalate*)

 #2: HDPE (*high-density polyethylene*)

#3: PVC or V (*polyvinyl chloride*)

 #4: LDPE (*low-density polyethylene*)

#5: Polypropylene

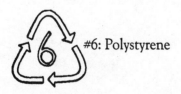 #6: Polystyrene

#7: Mixed plastic (*several types of plastic mixed together*)

OTHER PLASTICS

We've already talked about #1 PET (p. 34) and #2 HDPE (p. 36). Here's some information about other kinds of plastic:

#3 PVC or V (polyvinyl chloride)

• Garden hoses, plastic flooring, credit cards and shower curtains are all made of PVC.

• PVC is also sometimes used to make plastic bottles. But be careful not to recycle them with PET (#1) bottles.

#4 LDPE (low-density polyethylene)

• LDPE is the plastic used to make clear packaging on cassettes and CDs, plastic sandwich bags, and plastic grocery bags. Some containers are LDPE, too.

• Many grocery stores are recycling LDPE plastic bags. Next time you go to your local supermarket, ask about it.

#5 Polypropylene

• Plastic lids, bottle caps, straws, and some food containers are made of this plastic. It's generally not recyclable.

#6 Polystyrene

• All "styrofoam" containers—things like coffee cups and fast-food hamburger boxes—are made from polystyrene. So are clear, hard plastic food containers

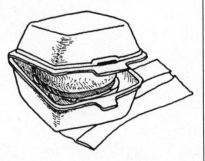

• It's technically recyclable, but few centers take it.

RECYCLING TIPS

• Most plastics still aren't accepted by recycling centers, so they wind up in landfills. This will change, but until it does try to buy products in containers that can be recycled in your area. Plastic with a #7 probably can't be recycled.

RECYCLE AT HOME

Okay, you're ready to recycle at home. But what do you do first—take out the bottles? Collect the newspapers?

Not necessarily.

In this section, we've put together five surprisingly simple steps that will help make your home recycling a big success... and a lot of fun.

12. GET TO KNOW YOUR GARBAGE

Take a Guess.
What are you likely to find in a garbage can?
A) *Your mailman* **B)** *Oscar the Grouch* **C)** *Paper*

Get to know your garbage? What's that supposed to mean—shake hands with a banana peel? Chat with a candy wrapper?

No. It just means you should take a good look at what's *in* your garbage...because before you can recycle, you have to know what you're throwing away.

What will you find in your garbage—soda cans? junk mail? apple cores? Is it all *really* garbage? Dig in and find out!

THE GARBAGE SURVEY

You can find out which recyclables you've been throwing away by doing a "garbage survey"—checking your garbage every day to see what's in it. Here's how it works:

1. First, decide how long your survey will last. A week is a good length, but just a few days will work, too.

Answer: C. Americans throw away more paper than anything else.

2. Now divide a piece of paper into four columns. Make a "Trash Tally" sheet like the one below. Then, if you can, make some copies on a copier machine.

Item	What Is the Item Made Of?	Is the Item Recyclable?			Recycled In Our Community?		
		Yes	No	?	Yes	No	?

3. Once a day, go around to each trash can in your home and see what's in it. Check in the kitchen, the bathroom, the bedrooms, and the wastebaskets in other rooms.

4. On your Trash Tally, list the things your family has thrown away. For example: Let's say you find a plastic soda bottle in the kitchen garbage. In column 1, you write "soda bottle"; in column 2, write "plastic"; in column 3, check "Yes" (on page 34, we said plastic soda bottles *can* be recycled). Don't put anything in column 4 yet. We'll do that in the next chapter.

5. Keep a new Trash Tally each day, so you can get an idea of how *often* your family throws different recyclables away.

Some notes:

• Don't worry about listing every bit of garbage. Your list doesn't have to be perfect—it just has to give you a good idea of what your family throws out.

• If you don't have time to keep a complete Trash Tally, just check the garbage every once in a while for a week, and make a simple list of some of the recyclables you see.

THE RESULTS

• After a week or so, take a look at your Trash Tally or list.
   ✓ How many things on it are recyclable?
   ✓ What recyclables does your family throw out most often?
• Now you know your garbage. Save the Trash Tally for later.

13. BE A RECYCLING DETECTIVE

Take a Guess.
Recycling centers can sometimes be found—
A) *In supermarket parking lots* **B)** *On school playgrounds*
C) *At fire stations*

I magine that you're a master detective. You have an important job: Your family wants to recycle…but they don't know where to go.

Where are the recycling centers in town? How many are there? What materials will they take?

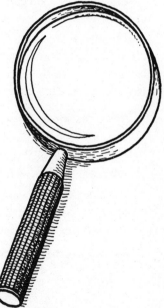

These mysteries must be solved before anyone can recycle…and *you* can solve them!

How? Do a little detective work. Follow the clues, ask the right questions—and you'll come up with the answers.

FOR RECYCLING DETECTIVES ONLY

Here are your Top 3 assignments:

Assignment #1: *Find out if your town has curbside recycling.*

• In some communities, trucks will come to pick up recyclables at the curb in front of your home. This is called "curbside recycling." Do you have it in your neighborhood?

Assignment #2: *Track down the nearest recycling centers.*

• If you don't have curbside recycling, you need to find places

Answer: All of them!

to take your recyclables. And even if you *do* have curbside pickup of some things, you may need to know where to bring *other* materials to be recycled.

Assignment #3: *Get the facts about recyclables.*

• Once you've found a recycler—whether it's a curbside program or a recycling center—you have to find out what materials they take and how they want their materials prepared.

HOW TO BE A RECYCLING DETECTIVE

1. Use your eyes.

• Look outside on garbage day. Is there more out there than garbage cans? Do you see boxes or bags or cartons of newspapers, glass, or soda cans? These clues could mean you have curbside recycling.

• When you ride around town, keep your eyes peeled for recycling centers. Check out supermarket parking lots for drop-off centers, look for signs, etc. If you find a center, take a look at the materials being collected there.

2. Ask questions.

• Want to find out if you have curbside pickup? Want to know where the local recycling centers are? Ask your parents … your neighbors…your teachers…or the garbage collector.

• If no one seems to know, try calling City Hall (where your city government is). Ask someone there. For the number, look in the *Government* pages in the front of your phone book.

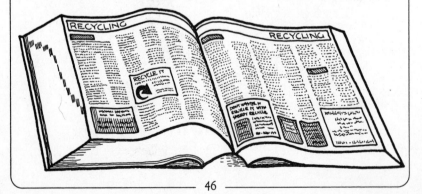

• To get the facts about local recycling centers, look in the yellow pages under "Recycling." Call the centers listed, and ask:

   ✓ Where they are and how you get there

   ✓ When they're open

   ✓ What materials they take

   ✓ If the materials need to be prepared or sorted in any special way

   ✓ If they pay for some recyclables (like aluminum)

3. Keep notes.

• As you learn things, write them down so you won't forget them. That way, you can share them with your family later.

• It's especially important to make a list of the materials that can be recycled in your community; that way, you'll have the information handy when you get around to deciding what to recycle at home or school. When your list is done, take out your Trash Tally (see p. 43) and fill in column 4.

• Now you're ready to start recycling!

14. DECIDE WHAT TO RECYCLE

Take a Guess.
How much time each day does it usually take a family to recycle?
A) *3 hours*   **B)** *30 minutes*   **C)** *3 minutes*

W hen you know what can be recycled at home and in your community, you're ready to get started.

But where do you start?

By making two simple decisions:

✓ What do you *want* to recycle at home?

✓ Who's going to recycle it?

HOW TO DECIDE

1. Get together with your family.

• Recycling at home can be a great family project. So why not have a meeting to talk about it?

Answer: C. Once you're set up, it only takes a few minutes a day to recycle.

• Share what you've already learned—why recycling is important, what recyclables your family's been throwing away, what you found out about recycling in your community, etc. Use your Trash Tally (p. 43) and your list of what's recyclable in your area.

• Ask if they're willing to help you try recycling at home. They don't have to make a big commitment—what's important is simply agreeing, as a family, to give recycling a try…and to stick with it for a certain amount of time.

2. Find out who wants to be involved.

• Remember: You can only recycle things if the people who use them are willing to help. For example, it will be hard to recycle steel cans if the cooks in the family keep throwing them away.

• Recycling at home is easiest if everyone works together. But if people in your family are too busy to help, you can still start recycling on your own. For example: Collect newspapers from around the house or recycle your own soda cans. When people see how much it means to you and how easy it is, they might join in!

3. Decide what to recycle.

• There are lots of things you *could* recycle, but if you're just starting out, it's good to begin with just one or two things. Once you get the hang of it, you can add more.

• If you're already recycling the basics—newspapers, aluminum cans, glass—try adding some new materials.

• See what you can recycle nearby. It's easier to go to recycling centers that are close to home.

15. MAKE A PLAN

Take a Guess.
Where can you store recyclables?
A) *Under your bed* **B)** *In bins, barrels, and boxes* **C)** *In a tree*

Help! It's the invasion of the recyclables! You've opened the door to recycling...and now they're taking over your home!

Bottles are piling up in the kitchen and newspapers are stacked all over the living room—where should you put them? A bag full of cans is ready to be recycled—who's supposed to take care of it?

There's only one way for your family to keep these recyclables from getting out of control: Make a plan!

HOW TO MAKE A PLAN
Here are three things for your family to decide on:

1. Where are you going to store your recyclables?
• Look for places that are easy to reach...but where recyclables won't get in the way.

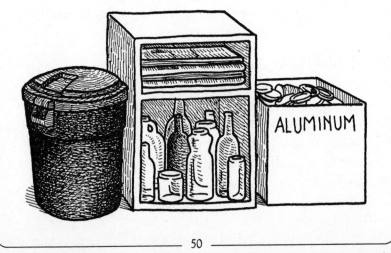

ALUMINUM

Answer: B. Or in any container sturdy enough to hold the materials you're recycling.

• Kitchens are good for empty bottles and cans, since that's where you usually use them. Is there room under the sink? In an empty cupboard? In a closet?

• If you don't have a lot of space in your home, you can keep a small storage container *inside* the house and a bigger one *outside* (on your porch, in the garage, in the yard, etc.). Every few days, you can empty the smaller container into the larger one.

2. How are you going to store your recyclables?
Recyclables can be kept in different kinds of containers. Which of these will work best in your house?

✓ *Cardboard boxes* are good for storing heavy things. You can get them for free at your local supermarket and recycle them when they wear out.

✓ *Paper bags* are good for storing cans and plastic, but not glass. Glass is heavy and can tear a bag open.

✓ *Recycling bins* are plastic crates made especially for recycling. You can usually stack them to save room. See if your city offers them for free. If not, you can buy them in hardware stores or from catalogs.

✓ *Plastic trash cans with lids* may be the best choice if people at your

---

51

house are worried that recyclables will look messy. Label trash
cans clearly, so no one thinks
they're full of garbage.

✔ *Other containers:* Plastic
laundry baskets, milk crates,
large or small trash barrels, or
buckets will also work well.

3. Who's going to do the recycling?

• Recycling at home works best
if you divide up the work.

• As a family, make a list of
things that need to be done and
see who wants to do them.
Here are some sample tasks you
might want to split up:

✔ Rinsing out any bottles
and cans that are left around

✔ Flattening aluminum cans

✔ Tying newspapers into
bundles, or putting them in
brown paper bags

✔ Taking everything to the
curb on recycling day

✔ Loading recyclables into the car, driving to the recycling center, and unloading them

• You don't have to stick with the same jobs forever. To
keep everyone interested, try trading jobs every month.

RECYCLING TIP

• To help everyone remember their recycling chores, put a
calendar on the refrigerator. On it, write down each job,
who's supposed to do it, and when it's supposed to be done.

16. TIME FOR A TUNE-UP

Take a Guess.
How do you tune up your recycling?
A) *With a wrench* **B)** *With a family meeting* **C)** *With a guitar*

C ongratulations! Your home recycling program is up and running...but is it running smoothly?

Just as a car needs to be "tuned up" regularly to keep it working right, your family's recycling plan needs attention, too.

So after you've been recycling for a while, it's a good idea to get together with your family to see how things are going ...and tune them up, if necessary.

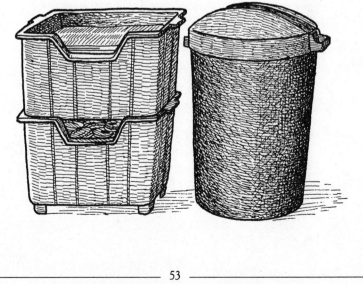

Answer: B. Recycling depends on people working together.

WHAT TO DO

• About a month after you start recycling, have a family meeting.

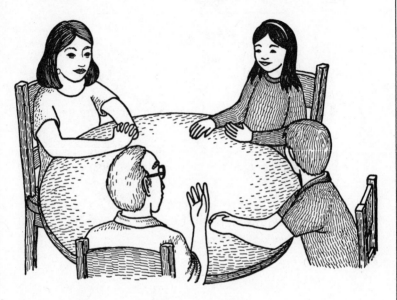

• Let everyone make comments and suggestions about how the recycling is going.

Here are some things you might want to talk about:

   ✓ Are things getting recycled as planned?

   ✓ Do you have less trash than before? How much less?

   ✓ Could you be doing some things better?

   ✓ Are you ready to add some new materials?

• Once everyone has made suggestions, decide—as a family—what changes or improvements you want to make. Then keep up the good work. (And keep up the meetings!)

REUSE THINGS AROUND YOUR HOME

R ecycling doesn't always just mean taking something to a recycling center so *factories* can reuse
the materials. Sometimes, it means finding a way to
reuse things in *your own home*.

By using stuff over again, you do what a recycling
center does—you save energy and resources, and you
cut down on garbage.

Here are five ways you can reuse things around *your*
home.

17. BE A PAPER-SAVER

Take a Guess.
*Your homework has to be on clean, neat paper. But not everything
does. What's a good way to use scrap paper?* **A)** *Write a poem*
B) *Write a note to your mom* **C)** *Write a letter to your dog*

Where's the first place your family looks when they
need paper for a shopping list, an art project, or a
phone message?

The kitchen counter? A desk?

How about a recycling bin or a garbage pail?

That may sound strange…but think about it. There's plenty of writing paper there—and most of it has one blank side, fresh and waiting to be used.

So here's an idea: Instead of throwing good "slightly used" writing paper away, keep it for notes. It's free…it cuts down on garbage…and it saves trees.

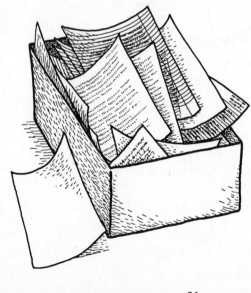

REUSING PAPER
The first thing you
need is a place to
keep your "used"
paper.

• One idea: Use a
small, open-top
cardboard box. Put
it in a closet, under
a desk, or any place
that's easy to get
to. (It needs to be
convenient, or no
one will use it.)

✓ Put an "X"

Answer: They're all good uses of scrap paper…but don't expect your dog to write back.

across the "used" side of each sheet of paper, so everyone will know it's "scrap" paper.

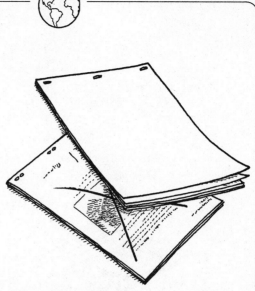

✓ Put the paper in the box with the blank side up.

• Whenever someone needs paper for a note or a list, they can take a piece out of the box.

• Or: When you've saved enough paper, place small stacks of scrap paper in useful places—near the phone, in the kitchen, on a desk, and so on. Then, whenever you need paper for a note or message, you have it.

• Or: You can make a scrap-paper pad. Here's how:

  ✓ Gather some pieces of paper that are all the same size. (You may have to cut them.)

  ✓ Find a piece of cardboard the same size as your paper.

  ✓ Stack 10 to 20 pieces of scrap paper with the *blank sides* facing up.

  ✓ Put the cardboard piece on the bottom of the stack. (It will be the *backing*, to make your pad sturdier.)

  ✓ Staple the whole thing together at the top...and you're done. You've made your own scrap-paper pad!

RECYCLING TIPS

• Not all paper makes good writing paper the second time around. The best choices: Notebook paper, computer paper, envelopes (for shopping lists), school papers (like old homework, class handouts, school flyers).

• Remember: Recycle scrap paper when you're done with it.

18. START A "SAVE-IT DRAWER"

Take a Guess.
What can you stash in a "save-it drawer"?
A) A bicycle   **B)** Your dog   **C)** A button

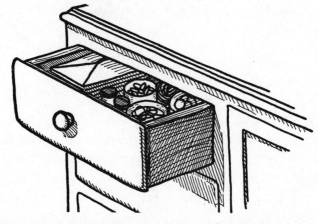

Paper clips. Rubber bands. Pieces of string. Safety pins. You may not need them now…but you don't want to throw them out either—because you *know* you'll be able to use them later.

So what can you do with them?

Set up a "reusables drawer" —a place to keep useful little items so you'll have them when you need them.

HOW TO REUSE ODDS & ENDS

1. Pick a drawer.

• Find a drawer in your home that's not being used…or find one that's full of "junk" already. In a lot of homes, there's a drawer everyone tosses odds and ends into. By cleaning it out a little, you can turn it into an "official" save-it drawer.

• Check with your family. See if they think you've picked

Answer: C…And anything that's small and easy to lose.

the right drawer. If not, ask them to suggest a different one.

• To keep things organized, use some small boxes and snap-top containers.

• If you can't find a drawer to use, try storing things in a cardboard box, such as a shoebox. Keep it in a special place.

2. Make a List

• What goes in the save-it drawer? Talk it over with your family. Make a list of what you want to save. (Then keep the list in the drawer as a reminder.)

• Here are a few things to keep in your reusables drawer:

- ✓ Shipping envelopes
- ✓ Film canisters
- ✓ Yarn
- ✓ Paper clips
- ✓ Twist ties
- ✓ Safety pins
- ✓ Nails
- ✓ Buttons
- ✓ Rubber bands
- ✓ String
- ✓ Screws
- ✓ Thumbtacks (put them on cardboard so no one gets stuck)

3. Save it...reuse it.

• Now, thanks to you, when someone finds a small "reusable" lying around, they'll know where to put it. And when someone needs one—they'll know where to find it!

19. PUT A LID ON IT

Take a Guess.
What can you do with a yogurt container once it's empty?
A) *Put it on your foot*   **B)** *Use it as a Frisbee*
C) *Store leftovers in it*

A fter your family finishes off the ice cream…when the yogurt is gone…when there's no cottage cheese left…what do you have?

Dirty dishes?

Well, maybe. But you probably also have a few reusable plastic containers.

They're perfect for storing anything from pickles to paper clips to Play-doh. So don't *throw* them out—*rinse* them out…and then reuse them.

CONTAINER FACTS
• People often think of plastic containers as "throwaways" or "disposables" because they come for free with the food.

• The truth is, they aren't really free—to you, because the cost of the container is added to the cost of the food, so your family is paying for it…or to the Earth, because making plastic uses up valuable resources like oil and causes pollution.

60

Answer: C. It'll keep your food fresh and help the Earth by cutting down garbage.

• And when you *do* throw containers away, you're not really getting rid of them. They'll sit in a landfill for hundreds—maybe *thousands*—of years, because plastic is not "biodegradable." So it makes sense to reuse or recycle them.

REUSING CONTAINERS

• The best containers are plastic tubs with resealable lids (lids that you can use again).

• What comes in these containers? Cream cheese, yogurt, whipped cream, margarine, cottage cheese, deli items, ice cream, sour cream, take-out food, and a lot more.

• Wash them out with soap and water when they're empty.

• Find a place to store clean containers—a cupboard, drawer, or shelf. Make sure your family knows where to find them.

• If you have no room for more containers, see who else might want some: A recycling center? Neighbors? Your teacher? Your art class?

REUSING TIPS

• Use the plastic containers to hold leftovers, bring things to school for lunch (see p. 110), or to store small items such as buttons, crayon pieces, or doll and toy accessories.

• Label containers so your family won't be confused about what's inside. Put a piece of masking tape on the container; write the contents on the tape with a pen.

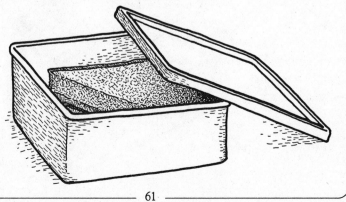

20. MAKE YOUR OWN ART SUPPLIES

Take a Guess.
If you lose one glove, what can you do with the other one?
A) *Feed it to your dog*   **B)** *Make finger puppets*
C) *Put mustard on it.*

Y ou've got newspaper spread out on the table. You've got markers, paper, glue, and paint. You're ready to create a work of art.

Now what you need is a box of recycled art supplies—egg cartons, yarn, pieces of wrapping paper, etc. They're perfect for making masks, collages, and lots of other projects.

You can have a lot of fun with recycled art supplies. So be creative! Start a "recycled crafts box" today!

REUSABLE ART SUPPLIES

1. Make an "Art Box."

• Find a big box for your recycled art supplies.

• Write "Art Box" on the side, so no one will mistake your treasures for trash and accidentally throw them away.

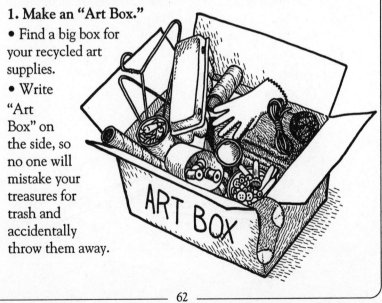

Answer: B. Well, you *could* try C, too, but B is a better idea.

- Ask your family to help keep your Art Box stocked with supplies. Here are some things to collect:

✓ scraps of yarn or string   ✓ clean yogurt containers
✓ beads   ✓ toilet paper rolls
✓ egg cartons   ✓ fabric scraps
✓ clean drinking straws   ✓ mismatched socks
✓ thread spools   ✓ clean popsicle sticks
✓ pie tins   ✓ corks
✓ cereal boxes   ✓ clean milk cartons

- If your box starts to overflow, you can give some of the things you've collected to a preschool or child-care group near you. People who work with little children can always use free art supplies.

2. Use your re-cycled supplies for art projects.

- You can make all sorts of things with recycled art materials. Here are a few ideas:

✓ **Plastic milk bottles:** Glue, tissue paper, and some paint or pens can change a milk bottle (or a bleach bottle or plastic water jug) into a piggy bank.

✓ **Steel cans:** They can be made into a totem pole, a pencil holder, or even a pair of walkie-talkies.

✓ **Egg cartons:** With glue, paper, and paint, you can turn an egg carton into a dinosaur, an alligator, or a turtle.

✓ **Cardboard:** The box that aluminum foil comes in can be made into a periscope, with two small mirrors. (Have an adult take off the cutting edge first.)

3. Save scraps at school.
• Talk to your teacher about setting up an Art Box in your classroom and collecting art scraps to put in it.

• You and the other kids can bring extra things from home to add to the Art Box.

FOR MORE IDEAS
• Of course, you don't need special instructions about what to make or how to make it. But if you'd like more ideas about projects, collecting materials, and using recycled art supplies in school, contact: The Scrap Exchange, 1058 W. Club Blvd., Durham, NC 27701. (919) 286-2559. They're a group that collects "throwaway" materials and makes them available to schools and kids for art projects.

• And if you'd like even more project ideas, we suggest these three books:

> ✓ *Likeable Recyclables*, by Linda Schwartz. (The Learning Works, Santa Barbara, CA)
>
> ✓ *The Recyclopedia*, by Robin Simons (Houghton Mifflin Company, Boston, MA)
>
> ✓ *ReUses*, by Carolyn Jabs (Crown Publishers, New York, NY)

• Look for them at your local library or book store.

21. A DROP IN THE BUCKET

Take a Guess.
What's a good way to recycle water?
A) *Use it to water plants*   **B)** *Take it to a recycling center*
C) *Send it to the president*

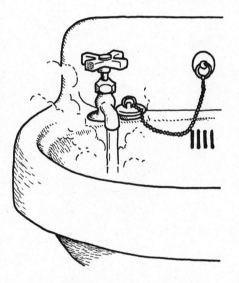

Time for a bath. Are you ready?

You turn on the hot water…but you can't get in yet—the water's still cold. So you have to wait…and wait…and wait, while it heats up.

Wow—look at how much water goes down the drain while you're waiting; there must be *gallons* of it!

Wouldn't it be nice if you could catch it and reuse it? You can! Here's how.

REUSING WATER

• Any time you have to wait for hot water—for instance, when you're about to take a shower or do the dishes—put a bucket or bowl under the faucet before you turn it on.

• Then turn on the water, and let it run into the container until the water gets to the right temperature (or until the container is full).

• Turn the faucet off for a second and set the bucket or bowl

---
65

Answer: A. Your plants will love it!

aside until you're ready to use it.

• Now you've got some water to recycle. You can use it on plants…to wash a car…to wash a bike…or to give to your pets to drink. You can even use it to wash out recyclable bottles and cans!

• The water left over in the pot after someone boils or steams vegetables has a lot of nutrients in it. Use it to water house plants—it's good for them. But be sure to let hot water cool down before you do.

WATER FACTS

• The average faucet pours out as much as 3 gallons of water every minute it's on. So, if you wait 3 minutes for water to heat up, 9 gallons of water could go down the drain.

• The reason it takes so long for water to warm up when it comes out of the faucet is that there's already cold water in the pipes. It takes a little while for the cold water to run out and be replaced by warm water.

WATER COMICS

Captain Hydro is a cool dude who fights water waste. Get his 16-page comic book, *The Further Adventures of Captain Hydro*, by sending $2 to: Innovative Communications, P.O. Box 23205, Pleasant Hill, CA 94523.

PASS IT ON

I f you have something you can't reuse, maybe a friend or neighbor can. Giving things way, or "passing them on," is an important way to recycle.

In this section, you'll find three ways to pass things on.

22. HAVE A GARAGE SALE

Take a Guess.
What can you buy at a garage sale?
A) *An old bathtub* **B)** *A skateboard* **C)** *An ugly painting*

If you've got a bunch of useful things to pass on, a garage sale might work for you. Just think of it…

Old paperback books, 50¢ each!

Old games, $1!

Old roller skates, $3!

People will actually give you money for your old things…and then they'll reuse your stuff, so it doesn't have to get thrown away.

That's why garage sales are so much fun—you get paid to "reuse and recycle"!

HOW TO HAVE A GARAGE SALE

1. Decide what to sell.

• Go through your house, attic, and basement. Make a list of things your family doesn't use or need anymore.

Answer: All of them. You never know what you're going to find at a garage sale!

• Check the list with your family. Anything on the list that someone wants to keep? Anything someone wants to add?

• If your family doesn't have enough stuff for a good sale, think about asking neighbors or friends to join in. They may have things they want to get rid of, too.

2. Getting ready.

• Decide where you're going to have your sale. Then pick a day and a starting time. (Weekends are usually best.)

• Advertise your sale. Make posters or signs announcing the place and time; put them around your neighborhood. Place an ad in the classified section of a local paper; most papers have a section just for garage sales.

3. Selling.

• Put price tags on all your items. If you're having a sale with other people, write their names on the tags, too.

• On sale day, lay out all your merchandise...and wait for your customers to arrive.

RECYCLING TIPS

• A garage sale doesn't have to be in a garage. In fact, people usually hold them in driveways, in front or backyards, or on the sidewalk in front of their homes.

• Garage sales are a good way for groups like scout troops to make extra money for special trips or projects. Everyone brings things from home or collects things from neighbors for the sale.

• You'll probably have things left over after your sale. Instead of throwing them away, make plans in advance to give them to a second-hand store (see p. 72).

23. RECYCLE YOUR READING

Take a Guess.
What can you do with a book when you've finished reading it?
A) *Make alphabet soup with it* **B)** *Give it to a friend*
C) *Feed it to your fish*

How do you recycle a book?

Can you put it in your compost pile? No, it will take too long to break down.

Can you take it to a recycling center, like newspapers or writing paper? No, the glue in the binding will clog up the paper-recycling machines.

Can you pass it on to other people? Yes!

You can take old books to used book stores, libraries, homeless centers, and hospitals. You can sell them at garage sales. And you can give them to friends who'll enjoy them.

No matter how you pass your books on, you'll be recycling some important resources—not just paper...but ideas, too.

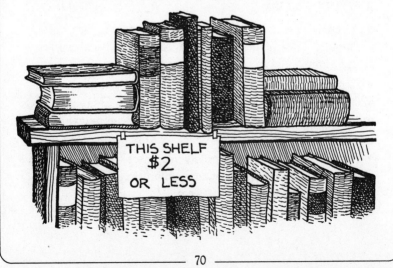

THIS SHELF
$2
OR LESS

Answer: B. And when your friend is done reading it, they can pass it on, too.

HOW TO RECYCLE A BOOK

• **Give it to a library.** Libraries always welcome used books. Many of them have special donation boxes where you can drop books off. Ask a librarian about it.

• **Give it to a homeless shelter...or a hospital...or a school.** These are all places where people (especially kids) could use more books to read. Ask an adult to help you call one of these places to find out if they can use your books.

• **Give it to a friend.** Better yet, trade books. That way *you'll* get something new to read, too.

• **Sell it at a used book store.** Used book stores may give you money for your book and then put it on the shelf so other people can buy it. To find a used book store, look in the yellow pages under "Book Dealers—Used."

• **Have a "Book Swap" at school.** Make it a class project. Pick a day for everyone to bring in an old book to trade.

RECYCLING TIP

• *Reading* used books—rather than buying new ones—is recycling, too. And there are two easy places to get them: used book stores and libraries.

24. PASS IT ON TO A SECOND-HAND STORE

Take a Guess.
Which of these is the same as a "second-hand" store? **A)** *A thrift store* **B)** *A glove store* **C)** *A store for left-handed people*

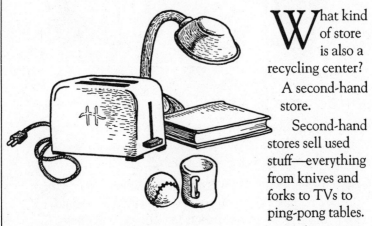

What kind of store is also a recycling center?

A second-hand store.

Second-hand stores sell used stuff—everything from knives and forks to TVs to ping-pong tables.

And every one of these things is recycled—because someone who can't use it anymore has sold or given it to the store to sell... *instead* of throwing it away.

If you have useful things that you don't need anymore, why not gather them and bring them to a second-hand store? Who knows...while you're there, you might even find some great reusable things for yourself, too.

RECYCLING AT A SECOND-HAND STORE

1. If you want to give things away:

• A *thrift store* might be the best place to take them.

• Most thrift stores sell things cheaply, so people who need the items will be able to afford them. Then the stores use the

---

72

money they make to help other needy people.

• Some thrift stores, like Goodwill and the Salvation Army, will pick things up from your home. Others will want you to drop the things off. Call to find out.

2. If you want to sell things:

• Some second-hand stores buy used items from people and sell them again.

• Other stores, called "consignment shops," will sell items for you and take a part of the money they make.

• Here are some different kinds of second-hand stores you can check out:

   ✓ *Music stores* often buy and sell used records, tapes, and CDs.

   ✓ *Used clothing stores* resell clothes that people don't want anymore.

   ✓ *Used toy stores* help kids sell their old toys. Any kid can leave a used toy at the store. If their toys are sold, the kids get half the money and the store keeps the other half. This is a new idea that's catching on.

   ✓ *Used book stores* may buy your books...or let you trade for others.

BE A RECYCLING DETECTIVE

• To find second-hand stores in your community, look in the yellow pages under "Second-Hand Dealers" or "Thrift Stores."

• Or look under the name of the item you want to buy or sell. For used clothes, for example, look under "Clothing—Used."

BE A SMART SHOPPER

What does shopping have to do with recycling? Careful shoppers already ask themselves questions like: "How much does it cost?" or "Is it worth the money?" before they buy something.

But if everyone adds the five questions in this section to their "shopping lists," we'll *all* be recycling—and *precycling*—while we shop.

25. Ask Yourself, "HOW LONG WILL IT LAST?"

Take a Guess.
What's a rechargeable battery?
A) *A battery you buy with a credit card* **B)** *A battery you pay for twice* **C)** *A battery you can use over and over*

Y ou see the signs in every store: Save Now!…Big Savings!…Save, Save, Save!

They're talking about money, of course. But if you're into the "Three R's," you can save a lot more than dollars and cents when you shop.

By buying things that can be used over and over instead of disposables that are thrown out after one use, and by looking for things that will last instead of breaking right away, you'll save precious natural resources, energy, and landfill space.

And that's worth shopping for.

BE A RECYCLING DETECTIVE
Here are two things to look for when you're shopping:

1. Reusables
• Think: "Reusable, not disposable."
• That means picking products made to be used over and over—anything from plastic popsicle sticks (to use when you make home-made popsicles) to rechargeable batteries.

Answer: C. More and more companies are making them.

2. Things that last

• Unfortunately, it's not always easy to tell if an item is "made to last." That's because to sell things, companies put a lot of effort into making things *look* good on store shelves.

• But a smart shopper will try to tell the difference between "good looks" and real quality.

• Here are some clues to look for:

✓ Look at the materials. Materials like metal, wood and thick plastic usually last a long time.

✓ Look at the parts. Things with lots of mechanical parts may break down more easily. Little pieces may get lost.

✓ Look for a guarantee. Many manufacturers will promise to fix their product if it breaks. That's a good sign—it means it's probably made to last.

Note: If you want some advice on picking things out, ask a parent or a salesperson to help you.

• Sometimes products that are reusable or well-made cost a little bit more. But they're often worth the extra money. Why? Because you can use them for a long time, so you don't have to keep on replacing them. And after you're done with them, you can sell them or pass them on to other people.

26. Ask Yourself, "IS IT MADE OUT OF RECYCLED MATERIALS?"

Take a Guess.
How can you tell if a cereal box is made from recycled paper?
A) *It's full of holes*   **B)** *It's gray on the inside*
C) *The picture on the front is upside down*

Congratulations! You've taken your cans and bottles to a recycling center. Now how about buying them back? What? Is that a joke?

Not at all. Taking your materials to a recycling center is just the *beginning* of the recycling process. Those materials won't *really* be recycled until companies use them again to make new things…and people buy them.

This is called "closing the loop," because it turns recycling into a circle. Here's how it works:

You bring paper, cans, and other recyclables to a recycling center.

People buy the new products… use them…and recycle them— and the whole loop starts again.

The recycling center sells them to factories.

Factories use them to make new products.

Answer: B. But if it's white on the inside, it's probably made from new paper.

Buying products made from recycled materials is one of the most important things you and your family can do to support recycling. If everyone buys recycled products, more and more things will be made of recycled materials.

BUYING RECYCLED

• You might be surprised at how many things are already made out of recycled material: paper towels, baseball bats, tires, cans, writing paper, skateboards, and much more.

• How do you find them? Well, it's easy with some products, which are almost always made from recycled materials. When you buy soda in a can, for example, you can be pretty sure the can's made from recycled aluminum.

• But finding out about other things—paper, for example—is harder. You may have to do a little investigating.

BE A RECYCLING DETECTIVE

Some tips for finding products made from recycled materials:

1. Look for this symbol on a package. It usually means something is made of recycled materials.

• But look carefully. Sometimes the symbol means the package itself—and not the product—is made from recycled materials. This symbol on a toy box, for example, probably means the *box* is made of recycled paperboard.

2. Look for the words: "Made of Recycled Material" on a product or package. Sometimes manufacturers use them instead of—or with—the symbol.

• Also look for "Post-consumer." It means a company has used materials that someone like *you* has recycled.

27. Ask Yourself, "IS IT RECYCLABLE?"

Take a Guess.
Which of these is recyclable?
A) *Your birthday* **B)** *A ghost* **C)** *A cat food can*

You're in the supermarket, shopping for groceries with your family...and it's your job to go pick out the ketchup.

A simple job? Guess again.

There may be 19 kinds of ketchup bottles on the shelves! Big ones, little ones, wide ones, thin ones...

There's also a choice between bottles made of glass and bottles made of plastic. How do you choose between *them?*

One way is to pick out a bottle you *know* you can recycle.

In fact, if you really want to save resources and cut down on garbage, that's a good rule to follow with *all* the things you buy.

ABOUT RECYCLABLES

• What's a "recyclable" package or product?

• Many companies will call a product "recyclable" if there's *some* way to recycle it *somewhere* in the world.

• But other people say that a product is only recyclable if

Answer: C. Cat food cans are made of steel and aluminum.

there's a way to recycle it someplace in their community.

• In a way, they're both right. But it doesn't help the Earth to buy a "recyclable" product you can't recycle.

• For example: In theory, almost all plastic is recyclable—but if your town doesn't recycle a certain kind of plastic, it will just wind up in the garbage.

• So ask yourself, "Can I recycle this in my community?" before you buy something that's labeled "recyclable."

BE A RECYCLING DETECTIVE
You and your family won't always be able to buy things made of materials that can be recycled. But if you want to try, here are a couple of tips.

1. Look for things you can recycle locally.

Generally, this means items that come in glass, aluminum, paper packaging, or some plastics. To be sure, use your "Recycling Detective" list of local recyclables (see p. 45).

2. Look for the word "Recyclable" on a product or package.

3. Look for the Recyclable symbol.

• Along with the word "Recyclable," companies sometimes use this symbol, which looks like the *Recycled* symbol (see p. 78).

• Look carefully, though—the colors are different. The arrows on the *Recyclable* symbol are dark, with no background. The arrows on the *Recycled* symbol are light, with a dark background.

28. Ask Yourself, "HOW IS IT PACKAGED?"

Take a Guess.
What do Americans throw away the most?
A) *Packaging*   **B)** *Spinach*   **C)** *Toothpicks*

Next time you're in a store, take a look around. You'll see that almost everything they're selling is either packed in a container or wrapped in paper or plastic.

Unfortunately, most of that packaging goes into landfills. In fact, about 1/3 of all packaging is thrown away *right after it's opened!*

Of course, sometimes there's no way around it—you have to buy something in extra packaging to get what you want.

But often, by making smart choices *before* you buy, you and your family can pick products that have less packaging to throw away. That's called "*precycling.*" It's a great way to save landfill space and cut down the amount of resources we use up.

HOW TO PRECYCLE

Here are four shopping tips:

Answer: A. As much as half of what an average American throws out is packaging.

1. See how much packaging is used on a product.

✓ *If you can, pick products with very little—or no—packaging.* This is especially useful to remember when you're making a choice between two similar products. Some pens, for example, come attached to a card and wrapped in plastic. Other pens are sold without any packaging. If they're about the same, why not pick one with no packaging?

✓ *Just say "No" to overpackaging.* Send a message to companies that are trying to sell you packaging instead of a product. For example: Sometimes, to make a product look better, they wrap it in one layer of packaging, like a cardboard box...then again in something else, like plastic wrap...and then, on top of that, they put it in a plastic bag.

2. If you can, buy in bulk. Buying one large container instead of a lot of little ones means less packaging to throw out.

3. Buy things in packaging that can be recycled. The more packaging you can recycle, the less you'll have to throw away (see p. 79).

4. Buy things in packaging made of recycled materials. Many items come in recycled packaging (see p. 77).

29. Ask Yourself, "DO I NEED A BAG?"

Take a Guess.
What resource do you need to make a plastic bag?
A) Oil   B) Mini marshmallows   C) Old shoes

D id you ever stop to think how weird it is that everything we buy gets put in bags?...Even when it's only
one item, like a candy bar or a bag of chips?

A bag in a bag—
sounds crazy...but it
happens all the time.
And then we just
throw the bag away.

What a waste!
Bags are made from
important resourc-
es—paper bags are
made out of trees,
plastic bags are made from oil...and manufacturing either
kind of bag adds a lot of pollution to the environment.

But you can help keep bags out of the garbage—just say no
to bags you don't need...or save and reuse bags you already
have.

HOW TO REUSE BAGS
• When you go shopping with a parent, take some paper bags
with you. At the check-out counter, ask the clerk to put your
groceries in the reused bags.
• Some stores now offer a discount for people who reuse
their own bags. For every bag reused, they give money

Answer: A. Plastic starts out as oil or natural gas—both "non-renewable" resources.

back—usually about five cents for each bag.

• You can also use your bags to carry other things—for example, to carry toys to a friend's house or take home books from the library.

STORING BAGS

• Pick a spot in your home to store bags—a drawer in the kitchen...a corner in the garage...a closet in the hallway. If you keep them near the front door, it's easier to remember to take them to the store. Keep some bags in the car for trips to the supermarket.

• When someone in your family brings home a bag from the store, save it and put it in your storage spot. If it's a plastic bag, you can wash it out with soap and water, and hang it out to dry.

• After bags wear out, recycle them. Brown paper bags can sometimes be recycled with cardboard (see p. 26). Plastic bags can sometimes be recycled at grocery stores.

SHOPPING TIP

• Another easy way to avoid throwing away disposable bags is not to use them at all! Instead, take along a backpack or cloth bag when you go shopping.

RECYCLE
IN YOUR OWN
BACKYARD

Y ou don't need a factory or a recycling center to turn banana peels, egg shells, and grass clippings into something useful. All you need is a little space outdoors, and a little help from mother nature.

30. LEARN ABOUT COMPOSTING

Take a Guess.
What happens if you bury an orange?
A) *It turns the dirt orange* **B)** *It asks for a glass of water*
C) *It becomes a part of the Earth*

Now, we'd like to show you one of nature's most amazing tricks...the incredible "Disappearing Garbage" act!

Here's how it works: Nature makes food scraps, leaves, and grass clippings seem to disappear...and a rich soil that can be used to feed plants appears in its place.

This recycling magic is called *composting*...and you can help make it happen.

NOW YOU SEE IT, NOW YOU DON'T
If you want to see the incredible "Disappearing Garbage" act work, here's an experiment to try:

What you need.
- ✓ A lettuce leaf
- ✓ A small shovel

What to do.
1. Find a spot where it's okay to dig a hole.

Answer: C. That's what composting is all about.

2. Dig a hole in the ground about six inches deep.

3. Put the lettuce in the hole and then fill it back up with dirt.

4. Mark the spot where the hole was. (That way you'll be able to find it again.)

5. Wait a few weeks, then go back and dig out the hole again.

6. What will you find? Not the lettuce—it will have become part of the earth. That means you've recycled "garbage" into plant food that could help a nearby tree or flower grow.

Congratulations!

31. RECYCLE LEFTOVER FOOD

Take a Guess.
What do you get when you recycle an apple core?
A) *An orange peel* **B)** *An apple pie* **C)** *Plant food*

A banana peel, an apple core, a half-eaten piece of bread.. This kind of garbage can't *really* be recycled, can it?

Sure it can. In fact, the Earth recycles it naturally all the time.

DID YOU KNOW

• Food can be composted because tiny creatures called *microorganisms*, that live in the soil, break down leftover food into tiny pieces that plants can take up through their roots.

• But this natural recycling process only occurs when the food scraps are in a place that has the right amounts of air and water.

•A compost pile is that kind of place…but a landfill *isn't*. In fact, food scraps have been dug out of landfills 20 or 30 years after they were first buried—and they look the same as when they were thrown away!

Answer: C. It happens in nature all the time.

HOW TO RECYCLE FOOD SCRAPS

• *To recycle food, you need a compost pile (p. 93) or worm box (p. 94). A few tips:*

• You can recycle most food scraps. However, meat, cheese, and other things with lots of fat in them should be thrown away. They don't break down quickly like other foods do, and can attract pests.

• To store food scraps: Keep a plastic container near the sink in your kitchen. Put fruit and vegetable scraps in it instead of throwing them away. It's a good idea to use a container with a tight-fitting lid, such as a large yogurt jar or a small garbage pail. It keeps the smell of old food from becoming a problem.

• When the container gets full, empty it into your compost bin or worm box.

32. RECYCLE YARD WASTE

Take a Guess.
Which of these makes good compost?
A) *Your old sneakers*   **B)** *A videocassette*   **C)** *A pile of leaves*

Do you ever have to mow the lawn or rake leaves at your house?

It's a lot of work, isn't it? And when you're done, all you've got is a big pile of leaves or grass clippings to toss in the garbage.

Actually, you have something else, too—plant food. Leaves and grass clippings can be composted.

DID YOU KNOW

• A whopping one-fifth of all garbage that Americans throw away is "yard waste"—grass, leaves, and branches.

• If this yard waste were left out where air and water could get to it, it would eventually turn into soil.

• But most of it winds up buried in landfills. So it will never becomes a part of the Earth again…unless you put it in a compost pile.

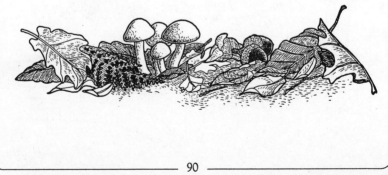

Answer: C. Leaves, branches, and grass clippings all make great compost.

HOW TO RECYCLE YARD WASTE

1. At home or school

• Make a compost pile (see p. 93).

2. Use a community compost program

• If you don't have room or time for a compost pile at home, your family may be able to recycle garden or yard waste in a community compost pile.

• This is a public place, sponsored by a local government, where people can bring yard waste to be composted. Towns often sell the compost or use it in local parks.

• Not every town has a community compost program. To find out if yours does, call City Hall and ask for the "Public Works Department." They should know if there's a program in your community. Ask an adult for help if you need it.

33. COMPOSTING PROJECTS

Take a Guess.
Where's a good place for a compost pile?
A) *In a swimming pool*   **B)** *In a backyard*   **C)** *In a living room*

H ere are two ways you can try composting at home: in a flowerpot, and with a compost pile.

MAKE FLOWERPOT COMPOST

What You'll Need
• A large flowerpot
• Enough dirt to fill the pot halfway
• One large trash bag
• Some food scraps

What to Do
1. Fill the flowerpot about 1/4 full of soil. Then add some food scraps until the pot is half full.

• What kind of food scraps? Vegetable peels, bread crusts, apple cores, leftover salad, etc. *Don't* add meat, dairy

Answer: B. In a backyard, or anywhere outdoors where you have the space.

products (milk, cheese, etc.), or foods with lots of fat in them.

• Cover the mixture with a thin layer of soil. This helps keep it from smelling, and keeps pests away.

2. Set the pot outdoors—on a fire escape, a balcony, a porch, or wherever you can find a spot.

3. Cover the pot with the trash bag.

4. Stir your compost mixture every few days or so with a small shovel or large spoon. This is important because it lets air into the mixture. Microorganisms need air to keep working.

5. Every few days add a little water to the pot, to keep everything damp. Don't add too much—you want your compost moist, but not soaked.

6. Gradually, the food will turn into soil. When the food has completely disappeared, your compost is ready. Put a plant in the pot and watch it grow!

MAKE A COMPOST PILE

• If you like the idea of composting, you might want to start a compost pile—a permanent place in your yard to turn your family's food scraps and yard waste into soil.

• There's a lot to know about compost piles. Here are a few people you can get in touch with to learn more on your own:

✓ **Your local nursery or garden center.** They often have good advice and may have books about composting.

✓ **Your local library,** for books on composting.

✓ **Your local recycling center or local environmental groups** may have information on composting.

✓ **Your local government.** Try the "Office of Solid Waste Management." Their number should be in the "Government" pages in the front of your phone book.

✓ **Ecology Action.** For $3, they'll send a guide called "The Simple Art of Home Composting." Write to: Ecology Action, P.O. Box 1188, Santa Cruz, CA 95061.

34. SET UP A WORM BOX

Take a Guess.
What do the worms you keep in a "worm box" eat every day?
A) *76 tiny pepperoni pizzas*   **B)** *A very small order of fries*
C) *More than half their weight in food scraps*

I s there anything you can do with food scraps if you don't have room for a compost pile?

Well, you could feed them to the worms.

Worms? Get serious.

No, really. Believe it or not, worms are some of the best composters in the world. They'll eat all sorts of food scraps—everything from potato peels to pancakes—and turn it into compost.

Sound interesting? You can see it for yourself by setting up a "worm box."

WHAT'S A WORM BOX?

• A worm box is like a miniature compost pile. It's a container (about the size of a bag of groceries) filled with

Answer: A. No, just kidding. It's C.

worms that recycle food scraps.

• You can set up a worm box in an attic, in a basement, on a balcony, on a patio or anywhere else where it doesn't get too cold during the winter, or too hot in the summer.

WHAT YOU'LL NEED

• A box about two feet wide, two feet long and one foot deep. You can make your own box out of wood (experts say wood works best), but you can also use a plastic tub. In the bottom of the box, drill lots of 1/2-inch holes—about one every 3-4 inches.

• Something to raise the box off the ground,—bricks, pieces of wood, etc.—so air can get in through the holes.

• You might need a "spill tray" underneath the box.

• Newspaper

• Two handfuls of soil

• A plastic garbage bag

• Some red worms. These are different than regular earth-worms—you can buy them at a nursery or a bait shop.

• Food scraps from your kitchen

HOW TO SET UP A WORM BOX

1. Tear sections of newspaper into strips about one inch wide. Soak the newspaper until it's a little soggy.

2. Put the shredded newspaper into the box. (You can put in as much paper as you want.)

3. Add a handful of soil.

4. Mix everything together.

5. Add the redworms to the box. One pound of worms (about 1,000 of them!) is a good amount to start with.

6. Cut a rectangle out of an empty plastic garbage bag. The rectangle should be just a little smaller than the inside of the worm box. This is the top, or cover, of the worm box.

7. Lay the plastic rectangle on top of newspaper bedding in the box. This will keep the worm box moist and protect the worms so they don't get too much light. Make sure the plastic doesn't completely cover the box—the worms need to get air so they can breathe.

8. Once your worm box is set up, start adding food scraps:

✓ Lift the plastic top, put food scraps in, and cover the scraps with 2-3 inches of newspaper. Then put the plastic top back in place.

✓ You can put in just about any kind of plant waste—grapefruit rinds, lettuce, celery ends, and so on. You can also add table scraps—spaghetti, bread crusts, etc. But make sure you don't add any meat or bones—they can smell bad and are difficult for worms to eat.

✓ Chop up onions, and bulky things like broccoli stalks.

✓ When you add food for the first time, make it just a few handfuls. Then let your worm box sit for a week or two before adding more food. This will give the worms a chance to get used to their new home.

✓ Gradually increase the amount of food you give them. By the sixth week, you should be feeding them 4 lbs. a week.

9. After several months your garbage will become rich soil. Use the soil to feed potted plants, or sprinkle it on a garden.

FOR MORE INFORMATION

• **Flowerfield Enterprises** sells worms, Worm-a-way® worm composting kits, and the best books on the subject: *Worms Eat My Garbage*, and *Worms Eat Our Garbage: Classroom Activites for a Better Environment*. For info, write to: 10332 Shaver Rd., Kalamazoo, MI 49002. Or call (616) 327-0108.

• **Ecology Action in Santa Cruz**, has free worm box pamphlets. Send a legal-size self-addressed, stamped envelope to: Ecology Action, P.O. Box 1188, Santa Cruz, CA 95061.

BRING RECYCLING TO SCHOOL

R ecycle at school?
Sure. School trash is no different from house-
hold trash. You throw out paper…bottles…some
cans…some cardboard boxes—just like at home.

This section will give you some ideas about what
you can do to recycle at school.

35. CLASS TRASH

Take a Guess.
What happens to the trash you throw away at school?
A) *It's dumped in the teacher's lounge*
B) *It graduates at the end of the year*   ***C)*** *It goes to a landfill*

Okay, class—today's subject is recycling. Open your textbook to page...

What? You don't have a recycling textbook?

Then you can start learning about recycling the same way you did at home—by looking in the garbage.

CLASS-TRASH SURVEY

• Doing a "class-trash survey"—keeping track of everything your class throws away—is the best way to find out what recyclables you *could* be saving.

• No matter what grade you're in or how many people are in your class, you may make some surprising discoveries. For example: At Clearcreek School in Ohio, a third-grade class with only 9 kids found that they threw away 109 pieces of garbage in one day!

• They found out that they were throwing away everything from plastic bags to gummy bears. But the thing they threw away *most* was white paper.

• The class decided to start recycling white paper...and in three months they'd recycled 285 pounds of it!

Answer: C. About 80% of America's garbage goes to landfills.

HOW TO DO A "CLASS-TRASH SURVEY"

1. Get everyone involved.

• Everyone who uses your classroom should be part of the project—the students, the teacher, and the custodian.

• Decide how long your survey should last. A week is usually long enough. A few days is okay, too.

2. Set up your survey.

• Put a big cardboard box next to the class trash can. Label the box "Dry Trash."

• Make sure everyone knows the difference between "wet" trash (the gloppy stuff—food, paper towels, etc.) and "dry" trash (bottles, cans, plastic, paper, etc.). Dry trash should go into the box. Wet trash still goes in the regular trash can; most wet trash isn't recyclable (and it can get pretty gross).

• Remember to lightly rinse out bottles, cans, and any other food containers before putting them in the box.

• Let the custodians know you're doing a trash survey. Ask them not to throw away the "dry trash" you're collecting.

3. Study your trash.

• After a week (or however long your survey lasts), your class is ready to see what dry trash it has thrown away.

- Spread a few layers of newspaper or cardboard on the ground. Make sure you cover a big space.

- Put all the dry trash on one part of the newspaper. Remember to be careful with the glass.

- Sort it into piles on the rest of the newspaper. Put white paper in one pile, glass in another, plastic in another, etc.

- Now you can see what materials the class throws away most, and what you could be recycling.

- **Note:** If your school has a compost pile, you can survey compostable materials in a separate container.

TRASH MATH

Here's a chance to use some math to see how much your class could save by recycling your white paper:

- Put the pile of white paper you've collected during your trash survey on a scale. How much does the paper you throw away in one week weigh? How much would the paper you throw away during the whole year weigh?

- According to some experts, you will save the equivalent of one big pine tree and three barrels of oil for every 118 pounds of paper you recycle. If your class recycled all the paper it uses in a year, how many trees and barrels of oil would it save?

36. DO IT IN CLASS

Take a Guess.
What would you like to recycle in class?
A) *Your homework*
B) *Your homework*   **C)** *Your homework*

I magine a place with bins full of glass bottles…aluminum cans…and stacks of white paper, ready to be recycled.

Is this a recycling center?

Nope. It's your classroom…or at least it could be if you

had a recycling program there.

You can help make it happen by working with other students, your teacher, and the custodians.

Sure, it's a big project—but it's worth the work…
because it can make a big difference.

Answer: Good news—you *can* recycle homework. Bad news—*after* your teacher sees it.

HOW TO RECYCLE IN CLASS

1. Form a Team.

• The best way to get started is to get other people involved. Tell some friends about your idea. See if they want to join your team. See if you can make it a class project.

• Kids in class will probably be more excited about recycling if they know *why* it's important. So help put together a class lesson on the subject.

• It helps to create a class job called "Recycling Monitor." This person makes sure recyclables go in the right bins, keeps non-recyclables *out* of the bins, and lets the teacher know when the bins are full.

2. Decide what to recycle.

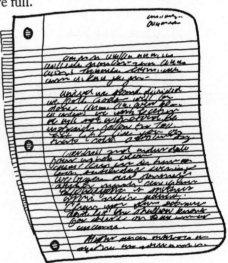

• Two important things to think about:

✓ What materials do you throw out most often?

✓ What can be recycled in your community?

• Your class might be able to recycle:

✓ **White Paper:** Includes notebook paper and computer paper. Homework, handouts, exams, and class assignments are often white paper, too.

✓ **Mixed Paper:** Includes construction paper, colored paper, paper bags, and paper towel tubes.

✓ **Containers:** Glass and aluminum containers used in class can be recycled. In some towns, you may be able to recycle plastic containers, too.

3. Storing recyclables.

• In some communities, the city government or a local recycler may be able to supply recycling bins to your class. Otherwise, boxes or empty trash containers will work.

• Storing recyclables in your classroom makes recycling easy. But if there isn't enough room, consider keeping them in the cafeteria or a storage room.

• Note: Make sure to let the custodian know about your recycling. Otherwise he or she might mistake your recyclables for trash and throw them out.

GET YOUR SCHOOL RECYCLING

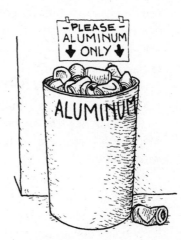

• Has your class already learned to recycle? Then why not try something bigger—get your whole school recycling. It's happening all over the U.S.

• For example:

✓ "Each week or so, the kids in Mrs. Eastwood's class go around to every classroom and collect old worksheets and notebook paper. Then, we load it into Mrs. Eastwood's car and she takes it to a recycling place. We don't get paid, but we get a good feeling because we know we're helping to save the Earth."
—*Leandra B., Seguin, Texas*

✓ "At Nevada Union High School there are 2 boxes in every room for white paper and colored paper. We also have dozens of recycling bins throughout our campus so we can put our aluminum cans in it to be recycled. We went from 55 dumpsters of garbage a week to 11. That saves us $60,000 in dump fees...enough to pay a year's salary for two teachers."

—*Glenda F., Grass Valley, California*

✓ "Our school has one recycling day during the week. We collect papers on Wednesday, and in exchange, we get free copies of *USA Today*."

—*Karen D., Oakland Illinois*

SCHOOL RECYCLING TIPS

• You'll probably need bins for different kinds of paper in each classroom and the office area, a bin for cardboard in the supply room, bins for bottles and cans in the cafeteria and the teacher's lounge, etc.

• There may be a law in your town saying that bins for recycled paper have to be fireproof if they're in school hallways. Check with your fire department.

• Make up a flyer explaining how recycling will work at your school. See that everyone at school (all teachers, school employees, etc.) gets one, and send copies home with students.

• Put instructions near all the recycling bins so that people know what to do, especially at first.

• Once your recycling program is rolling, think of a way to let people know how well it's working, such as colorful posters telling people how many pounds of paper, aluminum, and glass have been recycled.

RECYCLING RESOURCE: *Recycling in Schools: How to Develop Your Own Program* is a booklet with resources and a step-by-step outline on starting a school recycling program. It costs $5. Write to: The National Recycling in Schools Program, The United States Conference of Mayors, 1620 Eye Street, NW, Washington, D.C. 20006.

37. COLLECT CANS FOR A CAUSE

Take a Guess.
How can you raise money for something important?
A) *Collect play money*   **B)** *Collect cans and recycle them*
C) *Plant a coin in your garden and watch it grow*

Wouldn't it be great to earn enough money to buy a tree to plant for your school…or take a field trip…or make a big donation to save endangered animals?

Well, maybe you can—by holding a "Can Recycling Drive" at your school.

KID POWER
Here are three examples of schools that set up can drives:

•The kids at Midlothian Middle School in Virginia had a can drive and collected 125,000 aluminum cans in two days—enough to fill two trucks! They sold the cans for $2,000, and used the money to buy equipment for their science department—a VCR, a microscope, test tubes, balances, beakers, and other things.

Answer: B. A can drive is an easy way to raise money.

• Valley View Elementary in California had a can drive too, and collected more than 5,000 pounds of aluminum. Each class was allowed to spend the money it made. Some classes had parties, some bought equipment, etc.

• Every year, the students of Ocracoke School in North Carolina raise $1,000 by collecting aluminum cans. In one year, for example, they used the money to give a college scholarship to the high school senior with the highest grades, to make a donation to the Edenton Church Home for Children, to help buy food for a pony they adopted, *and* to pay for a field trip!

HOW TO PUT TOGETHER A CAN DRIVE

1. Plan before you start.
• Form a team. A can drive is a big project, so you need to get a lot of kids to work on it together. Ask your teacher to make it a class project.

• Pick a cause or project you want to raise money for.

• Get your principal's approval.

2. Find a recycler who will buy your cans.

• Call local recycling centers and supermarkets.

• Or call the Reynolds Aluminum Recycling Hotline: (800) 228-2525. They have recycling centers all over the country. Some Reynolds recycling centers even have special programs set up for school can drives.

3. Set up your drive.

• Pick a date for your drive. It could be on one day during the weekend or a few mornings before school starts.

Note: Choose your date carefully. You need to advertise early so everyone has enough time to collect cans. One or two months is enough time to alert people.

• Advertise your drive.

✓ Put posters and flyers up around your school, in nearby neighborhoods, and in the windows of local businesses.

✓ Send home notices to parents.

✓ If your school has a newsletter, advertise there, too.

✓ Tell the local newspaper about your drive, and suggest that they write a story about it.

COLLECTING THE CANS

• You'll probably collect thousands of cans, so you're going to need a big place to store them.

• One possibility: Ask your recycling center to bring a truck or large dumpster to your school on the day of your can drive. Then, when the drive is over, they can come back and pick up the cans.

• If the recycler won't pick cans up, get some parents with trucks or large cars to help out.

Note: It's better to collect and store cans outdoors than in the school. It's easier for people to drop them off *and* you don't have to worry about sticky floors or smelly classrooms.

FOR MORE INFORMATION
Reynolds Aluminum has put together a kit for schools interested in doing a can drive. It's called *The Aluminum Recycling Environmental Action Kit: Quick Tips for Starting Your School's Aluminum Recycling Program.* You or your teacher can get it by writing to Reynolds Aluminum Recycling Co., P.O. Box 27003, Richmond, VA 232261-7003.

38. RECYCLE IN THE CAFETERIA

Take a Guess.
What should you do when you're through with lunch in the cafeteria? A) Run out the door B) Take some stomach medicine C) Start recycling

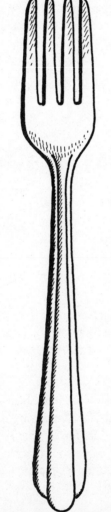

Banana peels…soda cans, glass bottles…cardboard trays…plastic forks. That's what you're likely to find in the cafeteria trash after lunch—and it's all going to wind up in a landfill.

What a waste!

Isn't there something you can do to help your school cafeteria throw out less and recycle more? Yes! It starts with a little recycling detective work.

BE A RECYCLING DETECTIVE
1. Check out your cafeteria.

• Next time you're in the school cafeteria, take a look around. Peek in the trash can, check out the lunch trays, etc.

• What are you looking for? Ideas about how your school could re-duce, reuse, and recycle more.

• Here are a few things to pay special attention to:

✓ *Cafeteria trays:* Are they

— 108 —

Answer: C. If all cafeterias recycled, it would cut down on a lot of garbage!

reusable or recyclable? Are they made from recycled materials?

✓ **Napkins and paper towels:** Are they made from recycled paper? Are they unbleached?

✓ **Utensils:** Are they reused...or thrown out? Are they recyclable?

✓ **Recycling:** Are there bins for aluminum and glass? Does the cafeteria staff recycle the steel cans and cardboard boxes they use?

✓ **Leftover food:** Is there any place to compost it?

2. Share your ideas.

• After your investigation, write down any recycling ideas you came up with.

• Then, see if you can get together with your teacher, your principal, the custodian, or whoever's in charge of the cafeteria to talk about recycling.

• You probably have many good ideas, but it's best to start with one simple project, like putting recycling bins in the cafeteria for glass and aluminum. Once that's running smoothly, other changes can be made.

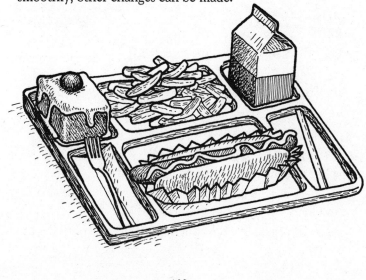

39. NO-GARBAGE LUNCH

Take a Guess.
What's the best way to take a sandwich to school?
A) In your pocket B) On a leash
C) In a reusable container

Lunchtime!
What did you bring today? A sandwich…an apple…
a package of cookies…
Anything else?

How about your brown paper lunch bag, your plastic sandwich bag, and the wrapper the cookies came in?

All of this packaging is part of your lunch, too. It's also part of our garbage problem, because when you're done eating, you throw it away.

Want to stop this waste? Learn how to make a "no-garbage lunch."

THE NO-GARBAGE LUNCH
A no-garbage lunch is exactly what it sounds like—a lunch that leaves you with no—or very little—garbage to throw away when you're finished. A few tips on making one:

1. Pick a no-garbage lunch carrier, such as:

✓ *A brown paper bag.* When you're done eating, save the bag so you can use it again the next day.

✓ *A lunchbox.* It can last for years and it will also keep your lunch from getting squished.

✓ *A reusable cloth lunch bag.* Make it yourself—be creative.

Answer: C. Right, a container you can wash and use again.

2. Sandwiches
• Carry your sandwich or other food in a reusable container. You can reuse a plastic food container (see p. 60). Or buy special food containers at the store.

• Wrap your sandwich in aluminum foil. Foil can be washed off and reused. It can also be recycled.

• Use a "ziplock" plastic bag. It's easy to rinse out and reuse.

3. Snacks
• Buy snacks in large packages instead of small individual ones—you get more food and less packaging for your money. For example, instead of buying lots of little bags of pretzels, buy one big bag. Then bring the pretzels to school each day in a reusable container.

• If you've got a compost pile, pick snacks that come in their own natural wrappers, like bananas and oranges. Save the peels and compost them (see pp. 86, 88, and 92).

4. Drinks
• Try carrying your milk or juice in a small thermos. Some lunch boxes come with a thermos already inside.

• Buy drinks that come in recyclable containers.

RECYCLING RESOURCE
Get more suggestions on packing no-garbage lunches by writing to: Center for Environmental Education, 881 Alma Real Drive, Suite 300, Pacific Palisades, CA 90272.

40. CLOSE THE LOOP

Take a Guess.
What does it mean to "close the loop"?
A) *Make your belt tighter*   **B)** *Tie your shoes together*
C) *Buy products made with recycled materials*

You've already learned how important it is for people to "close the loop" by buying recycled products for their homes (see p. 77), but have you ever thought what a difference it would make if schools bought recycled products, too?

Imagine, for example, how many trees we could save if your school—and every school—started using recycled paper.

You can help make it happen.

How?

By starting a "Buy Recycled" project at your school.

SCHOOL NOTES

• One reason more schools haven't started using recycled paper is that people think it isn't practical. They say recycled paper is too expensive, too hard to get, or is low quality.

Answer: C. It's one of the most important things you can do to keep recycling alive.

• But if those people took a better look at recycled paper, they might change their minds: more and more companies are making high-quality recycled paper at a reasonable price…and it's getting easier to find.

HOW TO START A "BUY RECYCLED" PROJECT

1. Be a recycling detective.

• Your school may already be using things made from recycled materials. To find out, look for the recycled symbol on supplies in your classroom (see p. 78.), or ask the principal or the custodian.

• Here are some common school supplies that are now being made of recycled materials. Your school could be buying them:

✓ **Notebook paper,** or any paper used for class handouts, school flyers, photocopies, class assignments, and so on.

✓ **Envelopes.** The school office probably uses a lot of envelopes, and they could all be made from recycled paper.

✓ **Books.** More and more books are being printed on recycled paper. In fact, the book you're reading right now is.

✓ **Paper towels, napkins, and toilet paper** are all being made from recycled paper, too.

2. Share your ideas.

• If your school isn't buying supplies made of recycled materials, you can help them switch.

• Ask your teacher to help set up a meeting with your principal.

• Your principal may tell you that products made from recycled materials—like recycled paper—cost too much your school can't afford it.

• If that happens, don't give up. Instead ask *how much more* it would cost. There might be a way your school could raise the money. For example, you could hold an aluminum can drive (see p. 105).

(see p. 105)

• Another way to lower costs: Buy supplies with other schools or other school districts.

• Take a poll. Ask other kids if they want your school to buy recycled paper...even if the paper costs a little more. Present the poll to your principal. Even if it doesn't get your school to change the kind of paper it buys, it will show your principal or the superintendent of schools how much you and the other kids care about recycling.

41. TAKE A FIELD TRIP

Take a Guess.
What can you learn on a recycling field trip?
A) *How glass is recycled*   **B)** *How recycling centers work*
C) *What happens at a landfill*

Can just one person really make a difference? Before you answer that, visit a recycling center with your class.

You'll find mountains of newspapers—more than you've ever seen; huge bins piled high with aluminum cans and truckloads of glass containers.

Just think, all of this might have been dumped into a landfill somewhere. But it's here instead, helping save our Earth's resources. How did it get there? People like you brought it.

It's a fascinating sight. But why stop there? There are plenty of places you and your class can visit that will give you an idea of how recycling works...and why it's worth doing.

HOW TO PLAN A FIELD TRIP
1. Investigate.
• Talk to your teacher about taking a field trip to learn about garbage and recycling. Let your teacher know you're willing to do some investigating about the places you might go.

Answer: All of them...and a lot more.

• Make a list of all the interesting recycling places in your community where your class could go. Whenever possible, look the phone number of the place in the phone book up and write it down on the list.

• Here are a few places you might want to put on your list:

✓ **A Recycling Center:** You'll see how recyclables are collected and stored.

✓ **A Landfill:** you'll see all the things that people throw away, including, unfortunately, many items that could have been recycled.

✓ **A Factory:** After your recyclables are collected at a recycling center, they are usually separated by materials and sent to different recycling factories or "material processors" to be made into recycled products. Visit a glass factory, a paper mill or an aluminum factory.

✓ **A Materials Recovery Facility (MRF):** Sometimes before recyclables are sent to a recycling factory, they go to a place called an "MRF" to be sorted and packaged. You'll see how glass, aluminum, and plastic are separated and prepared for factories.

✓ **Stores around town:** You can learn a lot just by checking out recycling in shops near your school. For example: Find out which stores sell recycled products, which stores collect recyclables, which stores accept recycled bags, etc.

• Show your list of places to your teacher. Together, pick out a couple of good possibilities for a field trip. Then your teacher can call these places to find out if it would be okay for your class to visit.

2. Help find a way to pay for the trip.

• Renting a bus to go on a field trip can be pretty expensive, so your class may need to find a way to raise some money to pay for it.

• One way to do that: Have an aluminum can drive at your school.

• Another way: Ask the PTA to help.

• Or, if your class can't raise enough money to go on a field trip, have the trip come to you—see if someone from a recycling center, a landfill, or a recycling factory will come talk to your class. Usually that doesn't cost any money at all.

• Another way to bring the trip to you: video. Here are two videos your class can get:

✓ **"Recyling—Your Next Assignment,"** is a video for grades 5-8 that follows the recycling loop of an aluminum can. Your teacher can find out how to get a free copy by writing to the Reynolds Aluminum Recycling Co. (see p. 107).

✓ **"The Original Recyclers: The Story of the Scrap Recycling Industry"** (video # 24974, grades 5 and up) gives you a glimpse of what happens when things like steel, paper, glass, and other materials are recycled. Your school can get the video on a free 5-day loan by calling 1-800-243-6877.

These companies have several videotapes about recycling available for sale or rent. Call for information or catalogs.

✓ **The Video Project,** 5332 College Ave., Suite 101, Oakland, CA 94618. 1-800-4-PLANET

✓ **Bullfrog Films.** P.O. Box 149, Oley, PA 19547. 1-800-543-FROG.

SPREAD
THE WORD

Y ou can recycle with a pen...a pencil...or even the telephone.
How? Use them to spread the word about recycling. The more people you tell about recycling, the more people will be talking about it, thinking about it...and doing it.

Here are a few ideas about how to share your ideas and information.

42. MAKE A RECYCLING MAP

Take a Guess.
When you see a number on a recycling map, you've found:
A) *A secret passageway*   **B)** *The Bat Cave*
C) *A place to recycle*

"Do you know if any recycling centers around here take plastic milk jugs?"

"What can I do with these old books?"

"What about these cardboard boxes?"

Your neighbors need help! They want to recycle, but aren't sure where to take their stuff. They'd like to buy things made of recycled materials, but don't know which stores sell them. They'd recycle their plastic grocery bags, but they don't know how.

You and your friends can make things easier for them.

How? By creating a special map that shows all the places in your community where people can recycle and buy recycled products.

HOW TO MAKE A RECYCLING MAP
1. Make a list.
• From the work you've done with this book, you probably

Answer: C. That's right, a recyling center or drop-off bins.

know a lot about places you can recycle in your community.

• So start your map by making a list of all the places you already know about. If you live in a big city, you may just want to list the places near your neighborhood.

• Don't stop with "official" recycling centers. Your list can also include stores that sell recycled products, such as recycled writing paper and recycled motor oil; places where people can get second-hand items, such as thrift shops and used-book stores; and drop-off centers (places that take recycled items if you drop them off).

• Add as much information to the list as you can about each place—the address, phone number, what it accepts, when it's open, and so on. The easiest way to get this information is to call the places on the phone and ask.

2. Use the yellow pages.

• You can use the yellow pages to find new places. Look under "Second Hand Dealers," "Recycling Centers," and the "Used" listings under subjects like "Clothes," "Furniture," or "Appliances" (Example: "Clothing-Used").

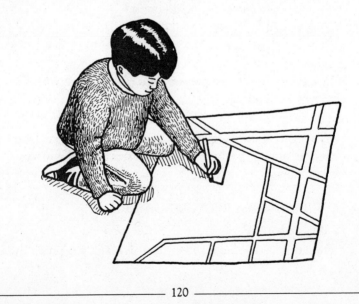

• Another way to use the yellow pages: Think of something that you know is recyclable, like white paper, then look up the places that sell it new—like stationery stores. Call to find out which of them sell recycled paper.

• Come up with some unusual ones. Is there a dry cleaner who can use wire coat-hangers? A packing store that takes styrofoam "peanuts"? A phone company that recycles phone books?

3. Number the list.
Put a number next to each recycler on your list.

4. Make a map.

• Now you need a map of your town or neighborhood. Call the Chamber of Commerce—they often give them away at no cost. Or you may be able to buy one…or make it yourself.

• Find each recycling place on the map and put its number there. For example: If Sally's Second-hand Store is number 2 on your list, write a "2" on the spot where the store is located. That way people will know where to find it.

• Together, your list and your map are a recycling guide that other people can use.

5. Pass your map and list out.

• Make copies of your map and your list and staple them together. Give them out to people in your neighborhood or put them in places where lots of people will see them, such as the library. The library might even want to give copies out.

• You can even send your map to your local newspaper, too. They might print it!

RECYCLING TIPS
In Albany, California, a student made a map of all the recycling centers in her town for a class project. City officials printed it and gave out more than 5,000 copies. If you'd like to see a copy of this map, send $1 to *Local Solutions to Global Pollution*, 1429 Bancroft Way, Berkeley, CA 94702.

43. WRITE A LETTER TO THE EDITOR

E xtra! Extra! Read all about it! Where? In the newspaper.

If you've got something to say about recycling, why not write a letter to your local newspaper? It's a great way to share your ideas with a lot of people.

But kids can't *really* write for the newspaper, can they?

Yes! Anyone can.

NEWSPAPER NOTES

• Almost every paper has a *Letters to the Editor* section, where letters from readers are printed.

• It's a way the newspaper gives people in the community a chance to share their ideas, opinions, and suggestions.

• Kids don't write to newspapers very often, so when they do, editors often pay special attention to them.

• Here are a few things you could write about:

✓ Why you think recycling is important.

✓ What you and your family are doing to recycle.

✓ What your school is doing to recycle.

✓ Tips on how to recycle in your community.

HOW TO WRITE A LETTER TO THE EDITOR

1. Get the address of the newspaper.

• Look for it in the *Letters to the Editor* section. They usually print the address at the bottom of the page.

• If it's not there, call the newspaper and ask for the *Letters to the Editor* address.

2. Write a letter about recycling.

• Here's a sample of a letter to the editor. Of course, you don't want to write the same letter. But you can use it as a guide to write your own.

> April 4, 1994
>
> Editor, Tenafly Bugle
> 112 Big St.
> Tenafly, Ill. 98650
>
> Dear Editor:
>   I'm writing this letter to make a suggestion. I think our town should put recycling bins in the park. Whenever I play there I see lots of people throwing away glass and aluminum containers.
>   I think if there were recycling bins, people would recycle instead. That would be better for the Earth, because it would save our resources and we would have less garbage.
>
>   Sincerely,
>   Jesse Javna

44. WRITE A LETTER TO THE GOVERNMENT

Take a Guess.
What do elected officials do with the letters they get?
A) *Eat them for lunch*   **B)** *Send them back*   **C)** *Read them*

What would you do if you were mayor? Start a curbside recycling program? Build more recycling centers? Sponsor a recycling fair? You probably have lots of good recycling ideas.

So why not share them, by writing a letter to the mayor? And why stop there? Write to your senator...your governor...or even the president of the United States.

All of these people make important decisions about recycling programs. To help them make the *right* decisions, they need to hear from people who care about recycling—people like you!

Answer: C. Elected officials take the letters they get very seriously.

KID POWER

• Do important people in the government really listen to what kids have to say? Yes! Here's one example:

• In 1990, a magazine called *P-3* started a letter-writing campaign to get people who worked at the White House to recycle. They asked kids to write letters to the president.

• Lots of kids wrote…and people at the White House noticed. In fact, they called *P-3* and asked the editors to tell their readers that the White House had started recycling.

WHAT YOU CAN DO

1. Write to your mayor or city council.

• Make suggestions, tell them they're doing a good job, or make a complaint if they're doing something wrong.

• For example: You might suggest that they publish and pass out a recycling map for your community.

• To find the address, look in the front of the phone book. There's a special section called the "Government" pages. Look for "City Hall." Call for zip codes, room numbers, etc.

2. Write to your state and national government.

• You can write to your representatives at the state capitol or in Washington D.C. to tell them your ideas and opinions.

• The address and phone number of your state representative and governor are usually in the *Government* pages in your phone book, too.

• Here are some addresses you can use to write to your government representatives in Washington, D.C.:

President _____
The White House
Washington, DC 20501

Senator _____
U.S. Senate
Washington, DC 20510

Representative _____
U.S. House of Representatives
Washington, DC 20515

45. TELL COMPANIES WHAT YOU THINK

Take a Guess.
What's an "800" number?
A) *The number of phones in a hotel* **B)** *The size of a really big telephone* **C)** *A telephone number that's free to call*

What would happen if a kid like you called up the headquarters of a big company to talk to them about recycling? Would they hang up?

No! Actually, they would probably be glad you called.

Most companies are very interested in hearing what customers have to say about their products. Many even have special phone numbers so you can call them for free.

So, if you have an idea for how a big company can cut down on packaging, or if you think they should get more involved with recycling…or if you just want to tell them they're doing a good job with their recycling efforts… find out if they have a toll-free number and give them a call.

HOW TO CALL A COMPANY

1. Find the number.

• Most companies put their "free" telephone number on the

packaging of their product. It always starts with "1-800."

• Look for it on the side or near the bottom of containers or packages. If the phone number isn't an "800" number, it's not free, so write to them instead of calling. Their address is probably on the package next to the phone number.

• Always get an adult's permission before making a long-distance phone call.

2. Decide what you want to say.

• Before you call, think about what comments, suggestions, or ideas you want to make. You can use what you've learned from this book to help you.

• One example: Suggest that a company use more recyclable materials in a product…or ask them to use less packaging.

• Your call doesn't have to be a suggestion or a complaint. You can also tell them you like what they're doing—and that you support their recycling practices.

• For example, if a product is made out of recycled materials, you could call the company to thank them and tell them you'll continue to buy their product.

• When you make your call, tell the company your name, your age and then tell them why you are calling. Be polite and to the point. Before you hang up, thank them for listening to

your suggestions or comments.

BETTER BRAND INC. ©
MADE IN USA
4421002

If you have any comments about our product, call 1-800-555-7777.

46. GIVE THE GIFT OF RECYCLING

Take a Guess.
Which of these things makes good gift wrap?
A) *Onion rings*   **B)** *Old balloons*   **C)** *Sunday comics*

Next time you want to give someone a gift, how about wrapping up a big, empty cardboard box?

Is that a joke?

No…it's a homemade recycling bin. It's just one of the creative ways you can spread the word about recycling.

When you give a "recycling present"—a recycling bin, something made of recycled materials, a book about recycling, etc.—you're giving more than just an object. You're also passing on your beliefs.

You're saying that recycling is important to you…and you want to share it with others.

KID POWER

This chapter was inspired by a letter to The EarthWorks Group from Mollie Clarke of South Carolina. Here's what she wrote:

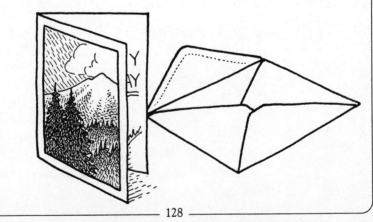

Answer: C. And afterward they can still be recycled with the rest of the newspaper.

• "For a Christmas present this year, I gave my aunt, my grand-dad and my family 'recycling centers.'"

• "I found different sizes and shapes of boxes at a local store and bought some cheap, but pretty, wrapping paper. Then I wrapped each box and labeled it with either a 'plastic,' 'glass,' newspaper,' 'aluminum,' or 'steel' sign."

• "This present was not only inexpensive, but it started my family recycling."

THREE WAYS TO GIVE THE GIFT OF RECYCLING

1. Give gifts that will help people recycle.

• Make your own recycling bins and give them to friends and family members.

• Give a recycling map (see p. 119).

• Give books about recycling.

2. Give recycled gifts.

• Gifts don't always have to be new. You can find great gifts at second-hand stores (see p. 72), or pass on something that's yours. For example, you could give someone a book you've already read. Include a note that says you're giving them something recycled on purpose.

• If you're buying something new, see if you can find a gift that's made with recycled materials.

3. Use recycled wrapping paper and recycled cards.

• When you get a gift, save the wrapping paper and reuse it to wrap another gift. Or, make your own wrapping paper. The comics section of the Sunday newspaper makes great wrapping paper.

• Lots of birthday and greeting cards are now printed on recycled paper. Look for the recycled symbol (see p. 78) on the back of cards. Or, make your own recycled card by using a piece of scrap paper and decorating it yourself.

RECYCLING PROJECTS

Here are a few "hands-on" ways to learn more about recycling.

47. MAKE RECYCLED PAPER

Take a Guess.
What can you make from old newspapers and a little water?
A) *Fruit punch* **B)** *Chocolate milkshakes* **C)** *Recycled paper*

The best way to find out how recycled paper is made is to make it yourself. We've reprinted this paper-making project from our other book, *50 Simple Things Kids Can Do to Save the Earth*. It's so much fun we wanted to make sure you got a chance to try it.

WHAT YOU'LL NEED
- Two and a half single pages from a newspaper
- A whole section of a newspaper
- A blender
- Five cups of water
- A big square pan that's at least 3 inches deep
- A piece of window screen that fits inside the pan
- A measuring cup
- A flat piece of wood the size of a newspaper's front page

HOW TO MAKE RECYCLED PAPER

1. Tear two and a half single pages from a newspaper into tiny pieces.

2. Drop the pieces into the blender.

3. Pour 5 cups of water into the blender. Using the right amount of water is important. Not enough water can burn out the blender; too much won't give you good paper.

4. Cover the blender (you don't want to have to scrape newspaper mush off the walls!).

Answer: C. It's surprisingly easy—and a lot of fun!

5. Switch the blender on for a few seconds, or until the paper is turned into pulp.

6. Pour about one inch of water into the pan.

7. Pour the blended paper (pulp) into a measuring cup.

8. Put the screen into the pan.

9. Pour 1 cup of blended paper pulp over the screen.

10. Spread the pulp evenly in the water with your fingers. Feels mushy, doesn't it?

11. Lift the screen and let the water drain.

12. Open the newspaper section to the middle.

13. Place the screen with pulp on it in the newspaper.

14. Close the newspaper.

15. Carefully flip the newspaper section so the screen is on top of the pulp. This step is important!

16. Place the board on top of the newspaper and press to squeeze out excess water.

17. Open the newspaper and take out the screen.

18. Leave the newspaper open and let the pulp dry for at least 24 hours.

19. The next day, check to make sure the pulp paper is dry.

20. If it is, carefully peel it off the newspaper.

21. Now you can use it to write on! Use it to make a card to go with your recycled gift!

48. PRECYCLE YOUR PARTY

Take a Guess.

What can you do to precycle your next party? **A)** *Invite just one person* **B)** *Dress like a clown* **C)** *Use reusable dishes*

Y ou're going to have a party?
Great! That means cake…games…presents…ice cream…prizes…and lots of other fun stuff.

But it also means a lot of garbage…because when the party's over, the floor is covered with party favors, paper plates, and wrapping paper. And they all have to be thrown away.

So what should you do—cancel the party?

Of course not! But you *can* precycle it. If you plan ahead, you can have just as much fun…and *save* resources instead of wasting them.

PARTY POINTERS

• Paper plates usually aren't recyclable. Once they are covered with food, they can't be mixed in with other recyclable paper and have to be thrown away.

• Paper cups are hard to recycle, too. They have a thin layer of plastic added to keep them from leaking. That plastic can't be mixed in with recyclable paper.

• Plastic cups and plates aren't much better. Most are made from polystyrene—a plastic that's not very easy to recycle in most parts of the country.

• So, one of the best ways to precycle a party is to avoid using throw-away plates and cups. Instead, you can use reusable plates and cups and wash them after the party.

• You can also wash and save plastic utensils. Lots of people

Answer: C. But we'd love to see you dressed up like a clown anyway.

throw away plastic forks and spoons after parties But they don't have to. Plastic utensils can be washed and reused later. It saves money *and* resources.

• Another idea: Get a set of reusable, durable plastic plates from a second-hand store and keep them in a box for parties.

HOW TO PRECYCLE YOUR PARTY

1. Use recycled invitations.

• If you're buying party invitations, make sure they're made of recycled paper.

• Or make your own, using scrap paper. Write a note on the back of each that says "Made of 100% reused materials."

2. Make recycled decorations.

• You can make party decorations out of loops of colored scrap paper, fallen leaves, leftover yarn, magazine pictures, and so on.

• Painted paper towel or toilet paper tubes strung together can be as colorful as streamers...and they'll let everyone know that you're serious about reusing and recycling! (Use them whole or cut them into sections to make them easier to work with.)

3. Reuse wrapping paper.

• Wrapping paper can be used again and again. So can ribbons and stick-on bows.

• You can also make your own gift wrap from scrap paper...or wrap gifts in the Sunday comics.

Note: After your party, put your decorations, reusable wrapping materials, and other reusable party items into a box labeled "Party Supplies"—and everything's ready to use again.

49. ADOPT A SPACE

Take a Guess.
What can you "adopt" that will help the Earth?
A) *A patch of wild flowers* **B)** *A grove of trees* **C)** *A vacant lot*

How would you like to clean up the Earth? No, not the whole Earth—no one can do that alone.

But you can clean up a little piece of it. In fact, there's probably a good place right near you.

Maybe you know of a vacant lot where people toss old bottles and cans...or a park where people leave trash on the ground...or a stretch of road or beach that's always littered.

Wherever it is, *you* can make a big difference if you choose to "adopt" it. By taking some time to clean it up, not only will you be making that little piece of our planet a nicer place to be, you'll also be collecting valuable recyclables that will otherwise go to waste.

Answer: All of them.

WHAT YOU'LL NEED

• Some garden or dishwashing gloves.

• Cardboard boxes or sturdy bags. (You can usually get boxes for free at a grocery store.)

• A recycling center that accepts aluminum and glass, and a way to get there.

HOW TO ADOPT A SPACE

1. Pick out a spot that can use some cleaning up.

2. Tell your family and friends about the spot. Ask them to help.

3. Label boxes or bags: "Cans," "Glass Bottles," "Plastic Bottles," etc., so everyone will know where to put each recyclable. You'll also need some bags for the things you find that will have to be thrown away.

4. Take the boxes or bags to your spot, and pick up as much litter and as many recyclables as you can. Wear the gloves while you're picking stuff up.

5. Remember: Stay away from broken glass or anything that looks dangerous. Ask an adult to help you with anything that looks sharp or heavy.

6. Take the recyclables you've collected to the recycling center and toss the rest in the garbage. (You'll probably need an adult with a car to help you.)

7. Go back to your cleaned-up spot and enjoy it!

50. RECYCLE
WHEREVER YOU ARE

Well, this is it—the last chapter. We'd love to share a few more recycling ideas—because there are lots of good ones—but we're out of room. So now it's up to you to use what you've learned and come up with your own ideas.

Just remember that recycling isn't something you only do at home...or at school...or at the store. It's something that can be a part of your life *wherever* you are. When you're riding your bike... camping out...playing soccer...on the beach...or anywhere else you're having fun, you can always take your recycling ideas with you.

And although this is the end of the book, it's really only the beginning for you. We know you're going to come up with more creative recycling ideas...and we'd really like to hear about them. Maybe we'll put them in our next book. So write to us and let us know how your recycling's going. Here's our address:

The Kids' EarthWorks Group
1400 Shattuck Avenue, #25
Berkeley, CA 94709

THE WRITE STUFF

Here are some comics, booklets and other materials you can send away for to learn more about recycling.

"The Scrap Map" is a fold-out guide showing all the details of how newspaper, aluminum cans, and scrap cars are recycled. It's free. Write to the Institute of Scrap Recycling Industries, Public Relations Dept., 1325 G St., NW, Suite 1000, Washington, DC 20005.

The Daily Recycler Wheel is a fun reference tool. You turn the wheel to an item like paper or glass, and it tells you recycling facts. Send $1.75 to Environmental Hazards Management Institute, P.O. Box 70, Durham, NH 03824.

Michael Recycle is a free comic book about recycling alumium for kids in grades 1-6. To get a copy, write to Reynolds Aluminum Recycling Company, P.O. Box 27003, Richmond, Virginia 23261-7003.

Recycling Times is a newspaper about recycling for people age 10 to adult. You can get it for free along with a package of materials about recycling by writing to: The Environmental Industry Association, *Recycling Times*, 1730 Rhode Island NW, Suite 1000, Washington, DC 20036.

The Importance of Being a Garbologist is a booklet for kids that's all about garbage, recycling, composting, and so on. Send $1.50 to Group for Recycling in Pennsylvania, P.O. Box 4806, Pittsburgh, PA 15206. They also have flyers called "Garbage Math" and "Composting in your own backyard" which you can get for free if you send a Self-addressed, stamped envelope.

"Recycling—The Every Day Way to Save the World."
You can get this free brochure by writing to: Environmental Defense Fund—Recycling, 257 Park Avenue South, New York, NY 10010.

Adventures of the Garbage Gremlin: Recycle and Combat a Life of Grime is a free comic book for kids in grades 4-7. To order it, write to the Office of Program Management and Support, U.S. EPA, OS-305, 401 M St., SW, Washington, DC.20460. To make sure you get the comic you want, be sure to write this order number in your letter: EPA/530-SW-90-024.

"The Great Glass Caper" is a brochure about recycling glass. Available free from the Glass Packaging Institute, 1627 K St. NW, Suite 800, Washington, DC 20006.

GENERAL INFORMATION
Here are a few more groups with information on recycling (although it may not be written especially for kids).

• *The Aluminum Association*, 900 19th St. NW, Suite 300, Washington, DC 20006

• *The American Forest and Paper Association*, Paper Information Center, 1250 Connecticut Ave. NW, Washington, DC 20036. Ask for information on how to make paper, and on paper recycling.

• *The National Association for Plastic Container Recovery (NAPCOR)*, 100 N. Tryon St., Suite 3770, Charlotte, NC 28202. Has information on recycling PET plastic bottles.

MORE BOOKS ABOUT RECYCLING

Here are a few books you can ask for at your library.

• **Trash Attack,** by Candace Savage. Douglas & MacIntyre Ltd, Firefly Books, $9.95. The best kid's book on recycling we've found. Engaging writing, entertaining illustrations.

• **Tons of Trash, Why You Should Recycle and What Happens When You Do,** by Joan Rattner Heilman. Avon Books, $3.50. Tells you more about how materials like paper, plastic and glass are recycled.

• **Cartons, Cans, and Orange Peels: Where Does Your Garbage Go?,** by Joanna Foster. Clarion Books, $15.95. Color pictures and lots of info about how recycling works.

• **Let's Talk Trash: The Kids' Book About Recycling** by Kelly McQueen and David Fassler. Waterfront Books, $14.95. A good book for young kids (kindergarten to third grade).

• **Reducing, Reusing & Recycling,** by Bobbie Kalman. Crabtree Publishing Co., $7.95. Learn more about worm composting, garbage craft projects, and ways to be a careful consumer.

• **Recycle, A Handbook for Kids,** by Gail Gibbons. Little, Brown & Company. $14.95. Big color drawings and some general information about recycling.

• **TRASH!,** by Charlotte Wilcox. Carolrhoda Books, $5.95. A very simple explanation of what happens to garbage, with great color photos.

FOR TEACHERS

*Here's a list of resources that can help your teacher get
the word out about recycling. Bring this list to
school and show it to your teacher.*

Don't Waste Waste! Environmental Action Coalition, 625
Broadway, 2nd Floor, New York, NY 10012. (212) 677-
1601. For grades 4-6. Includes a bibliography and a list of
additional resources. 20 pages, $4.

"The Great Glass Caper. "The Glass Packaging Institute,
1627 K St. NW, Suite 800, Washington, DC 20006.
(202) 887-4850. Six student activities about recycling basics, plus a wall chart about the glass recycling process.
Grades 4-6. Free.

**Garbage Reincarnation: An Interdisciplinary Approach to
Materials Conservation & Recycling.** GRI, P.O. Box
1375, Santa Rosa, CA 95402. (707) 584-8666. Teaches recycling and conservation principles through classroom and
community activities, including making your own mini-
sanitary landfill. Grades 4-6. $8.95.

**"Let's Recycle: A Curriculum for Solid Waste Aware-
ness."** Office of Program Management and Support, OS-
305, U.S. EPA, 401 M St. SW, Washington, DC 20460.
Grades K-12. EPA/530-SW-90-005. Designed to increase
students' science, vocabulary, math, and creative writing
skills. Free.

Recycling: A Solution to Pollution! Community Recycling
Center, 720 N. Market St., Champaign, IL 61820. (217)
351-4495. Simple and interesting for kindergartners

through 4th graders. Includes reproducible activity pages. $12.

Reusable Math. Pennsylvania Resources Council, Inc. (PRC), P.O. Box 88, Media, PA 19063-0088. (610) 565-9131. Math problems relating to recycling. Grades 1-8. Includes a teachers guide, $3.50.

The Fourth R: An Action Booklet for Recycling in the Classroom and School Building. Wisconsin Department of Natural Resources, Recycling Coordinator, P.O. Box 7921, Madison, WI 53707. A booklet written for grades 4-12. They also have publications called *Recycling Study Guide*, *K-3 Supplement to the Recycling Study Guide*, *Nature's Recyclers Activity Guide*, and *Nature's Recyclers Coloring Book*. All of them are free. (Note: They also have an environmental kit for $12.70 plus state tax.)

"The 4th R Recycling Curriculum." For ordering info, contact the City and County of San Francisco Recycling Program, 1145 Market St., Suite 401, San Francisco, CA 94103. A comprehensive guide broken into lessons on recycling, reusing, litter reducing, and getting the message out. Grades K-5. For teachers only.

The Scrap Map (Teacher's Kit), Institute of Scrap Recycling Industries, 1325 G St., NW, Suite 1000, Washington, DC 20005-3104. (202) 466-4050. A teacher's guide for using the map listed on p. 146. Shows students how newspaper, aluminum cans, and scrap cars are recycled. For grades K-6, $5. You can order the maps in bulk, too. A package of 30 student maps is $15. (For orders under $25, please include $5 for postage.)

Garbage Games, by Betty Isaak. The Learning Works, P.O. Box 6187, Santa Barbara, CA 93160 (800) 235-5767. A book of language and math worksheets that uses containers and boxes as materials. $12.95 including postage and handling.

Composting Across the Curriculum: A Teacher's Guide to Composting. Marin County Office of Waste Management, 10 North San Pedro Rd., Rm 1022, San Rafael, CA 94903. A 110-page booklet with 21 activities and resources. Detailed specifics about how to compost, how to make a worm box, and how to integrate composting into science, social science, language arts, and math curricula. For elementary school and up. $8.50.

NOTE: This material is just a partial listing of recycling materials available to teachers. For a more comprehensive list of all environmental curricula, we recommend contacting The Center for Environmental Education. They are an information clearinghouse specifically for environmental education materials, and have over 700 teacher-reviewed and approved titles to recommend. Their resources can be accessed by phone, mail, and in person.

The Center for Environmental Education
881 Alma Real Drive, Suite 300 C
Pacific Palisades, CA 90272.
(310) 454-4585.